T0195065

A Look From the Top
of Shénir Mountain

From the lions' dens —Song of Solomon 4:8

A Look From the Top of Shénir Mountain

From the lions' dens —Song of Solomon 4:8

by

Marilyn J. Dworshak

WESTBOW
PRESS°
A DIVISION OF THOMAS NELSON
& ZONDERVAN

WestBow Press books may be ordered through booksellers or by contacting:

WestBow Press
A Division of Thomas Nelson & Zondervan
1663 Liberty Drive
Bloomington, IN 47403
www.westbowpress.com
844-714-3454

Foreword – by Daniel J. Dworshak

Scripture taken from the King James Version of the Bible.

ISBN: 978-1-6642-1408-8 (sc)
ISBN: 978-1-6642-1409-5 (hc)
ISBN: 978-1-6642-1407-1 (e)

Library of Congress Control Number: 2020923467

Print information available on the last page.

WestBow Press rev. date: 01/13/2021

CONTENTS

Look from the top of Amana,
from the top of Shénir and Hermon,
from the lions' dens …

and from the mountains of the leopards.
—Song of Solomon 4:8

Preface

T he Lord Jesus Christ came down from heaven and wrote an autobiography like no other. His gift of salvation, penned in His blood, is one that no earthly man could ever write but continues to be written about today.

Each day Christian writers rise early and retreat to a quiet place to spend time alone with God in a season of thanksgiving and self-examination. While enjoying the sounds of the morning, they find their quills filled with lines of meditation. Even a sparrow, perched on the housetop, can be heard lifting a song of praise to its Creator in these first hours.

It is a joy to present <u>A Look From the Top of Shénir Mountain</u>—a devotional penned in such a setting. Each testimony is written using analogies, word pictures, poetry, or prose. Carefully gleaned scriptures are inter-woven to constitute a clear understanding of biblical concepts to lead the reader to recognize and respond to the Creator.

Before reading this book, I encourage you first to open the Word of God, where you will find strength and wisdom for the days ahead. As you lift your eyes, as it were, above the hills, may the Spirit of the Lord rest upon you like the dew of Hermon and your heart be touched to respond to His timeless invitation to become a partaker of His divine grace.

Lord,

May this book point us to the Word of God, where, with each turning of the page, wisdom and understanding are found perfuming the air with rich and enduring wealth. Speak to our hearts as we look up and proclaim: "The Lord is my rock, and my fortress, and my deliverer; my God, my strength, in whom I will trust; my buckler, and the horn of my salvation, and my high tower" (Ps. 18:2).

I will lift up mine eyes unto the hills, from whence comes
my help. My help comes from the Lord,
who made heaven and earth.

—Psalm 121:1,2

Foreword

We read in Genesis: "And Enoch walked with God: and then he was not, for God took him" (Gen. 5:24). Does this mean Enoch walked side-by-side with the Creator on the earth? I pray that I am able and privileged to walk with God, just as Enoch did.

To walk with God, we must have communication and closeness, first by listening to the Word through the Holy Spirit living in us, and then with thankfulness, letting our "requests be made known unto God" (Phil. 4:6) in prayer. In our human experience, the closer we are to a loved one, the more we enjoy a more intimate conversation, i.e., whispers of love and comforting compassion. In the spiritual realm, we must also be close to God so that these loving words may go back and forth; after all, God is full of lovingkindness. I like that great word found in many of the Psalms.

Joshua expresses this "walk with God" well, saying: "Take heed to love the Lord your God and to walk in all His ways; keep His commandments, and cleave unto Him, and serve Him with all your heart and with all your soul" (Josh 22:5). "Let him that glories, glory in this," Jesus said, "that he understands and knows Me, that I am the Lord who exercises lovingkindness, judgment, and righteousness in the earth" (Jer. 9:24).

We may not fully understand all things about God, but what little we do know is wonderful, bringing peace and satisfaction to our lives. Stop and appreciate how much God keeps giving His grace, mercy, love, care, protection, salvation, abundant life, peace, hope, and security. One can go on for pages and books full of pages with the language of God's interaction in our lives. "I can do all things," Paul said, "through Christ, who strengthens me" (Phil. 4:13). This is God's hand on our lives when we seek Him, hold on to Him, and depend on Him.

A Look From the Top
of Shénir Mountain

From the lions' dens. —Song of Solomon 4:8

A Faithful Friend

Most men will proclaim each one his own goodness:
but a faithful man who can find?

—Proverbs 20:6

Beams of sunlight peek out from behind a high and stony mountain; all is still until the silence is broken by the sound of a thrush stirring in the trees. The cedars of Lebanon spread forth their branches to protect her from the icy grip of winter's fetters, for they are the best of friends. It is rare to find such a friend who loves not only in word and tongue, but "in actions and in truth" (1 Jn. 3:18).

A faithful friend who can find—
one who walks with God
and has a servant's heart?

I know of one.

Every day she leaves her comfort place
and peddles down the road toward town—
past painted houses, sidewalk lights,
and things of no concern.

With tangled hair and bangs cut high,
she smiles along the way.

Her kindred heart loves simple things—
while sowing seeds of hope,
that fall beyond intent
in the quaintest shops and café stops.

A godly heart makes her face smile,
as her voice shares a prayer with all she meets.
Those who see her know she seeks nothing more
than just a godly word —or two.

Though a quiet girl inside,
she wears her faith out on her sleeve.
Full of revelation,
she has a pure and grateful heart,
and no one is a stranger.

Her thoughts are on the things of God,
and He is always by her side
while down the road she goes.

Even in the darkest hours,
she listens for His still small voice.
And yes, they, too, are the best of friends.

A Psalm Meant for a King

O Lᴏʀᴅ, our Lord, how excellent is Your name in all the earth!
—Psalm 8:1

A humble heart never wearies of its godly work or position of humility; instead, it finds itself at the feet of Jesus embracing servitude. Only there can we learn to share the love He first showed us.

Thus says the high and lofty One who inhabits Eternity, whose name is Holy; I dwell in the high and holy place with him also that is of a contrite and humble spirit, to revive the spirit of the humble, and to revive the heart of the contrite ones. (Isa. 57:15)

At Your feet, I come,
to sing a psalm meant for a king—
a song the angels sing
both day and night.

For praise, like love, should never fail
nor quiet from its ministry—
like Your written words:
"For God so loved the world" (Jn. 3:16).

I shall begin my song, O God,
addressing You as majesty—
Abba Father, Prince of Peace,
and Mighty God.

With grace upon my lips
and as penned by skillful writers,

I'll lift my voice and sing
the Song of Songs!

I'll sing of mercies new
that never cease and are renewed—
words an earthly man like me
could never write.

As joy and gladness fill my heart,
the hills and mountains shall break forth,
and sing to You, O God,
"How Great Thou Art!"

Then as the trees begin to clap (Isa. 55:12),
I'll sing that psalm meant for a king:
"O LORD, our Lord,
how excellent is Your name!" (Ps. 8:1).

A Straight Path of Decision

Blessed are the pure in heart, for they shall see God.
—Matthew 5:8

Who are among those who are blessed? Assuredly, they are the multitudes listening to Jesus as He teaches from the mountain of the Lord's house (Isa. 2:2). There before them sat the only begotten Son of God—the Eternal Word in the flesh and the light of the world (Jn. 8:12).

The blessing of seeing God is promised to those who are pure in heart. After bidding the people to the mountain, truth came to them through Jesus as prophesied by Zebulun and Issachar (Deut. 33:19). "Blessed are the pure in heart," He said, "for they shall see God" (Matt. 5:8).

My crooked paths are straight, O God,
and my mountains are made low.
My valleys are exalted
to make way for You, Lord.

Rough places have been planed
and stumbling blocks of sin, removed.
Thorns and briars are uprooted,
and stony places are now smooth.

Find in my heart's highway
and in the boundaries of my soul
a straight path of decision,
as Your eyes run to and fro.

If a crossing tries to block Your way
like a double-minded man (Jas. 1:8)
let the voice heard in the wilderness (Mk. 1:3)
call me back again.

When my appointed day has come
to hear the angels sing,
keep my feet from falling, Lord,
as I greet the King of kings!

Lord,

In prayer, we find strength and guidance; may it be a treasure to us, and may we never cease to delight in it. Teach us to pray more abundantly and more effectually, enabling us through Your Spirit to have a pure testimony, for only with Your guiding hand upon us are we able to gain wisdom which cannot come from any other source.

A Trial of My Faith

Behold, the day comes, that shall burn as an oven; and all the proud, yes, and all that do wickedly, shall be stubble: and the day that comes shall burn them up, says the LORD of hosts.

—Malachi 4:1

T he struggle between our flesh and our spirit becomes apparent when we decide to follow the Lord. When left to ourselves, our flesh lives in a way that seems right in itself, but when the Spirit comes to live in our hearts, every high thing that exalts itself against the knowledge of God is brought into captivity to the obedience of Christ (2 Cor. 10:5).

Believers who desire to follow the Lord "wrestle not with flesh and blood, but against principalities, against powers, and the rulers of the darkness" (Eph. 6:12). They would rather be a doorkeeper in the house of God than live in wickedness. Someday they shall dwell in His house and will never cease to praise Him (Ps. 84:4).

We do not have "a high priest who cannot be touched with the feeling of our infirmities but was in all points tempted like we are, yet without sin" (Heb. 4:15). Though our flesh desires to follow roads that lead away from the path of life, the Lord knows which way we will take and has made a way for us to escape. When we turn from our wicked ways, He is plenteous in mercy and ready to forgive us of the sins that leave us broken.

Faith brings our souls to heaven, and our afflictions are "appointed" (1 Thess. 3:3) unto us to try our faith, so that we may be found unto praise, and honor, at the appearing of the Lord Jesus Christ. Though we cannot see Him, we believe and love Him. Blessed are they who "passing through the valley of Baca make it a well; the rain also fills the pools" (Ps. 84:6).

Temptation's door needs not a key
to swing into an unsure place—
a place the Lord stood toe to toe,
yet did not sin (Heb. 4:15).

Wrestling not with flesh and blood,
we find ourselves near miry clay
at a place called
"What I would not,
that I do" (Rom. 7:19).

Bloodstained footprints of the King
cross the path we dare to go,
to remind us:
"Choose this day
whom you will serve" (Josh. 24:15).

He is acquainted with our ways
and knows the path that we will take.
This miry clay is just a trial of our faith.

"My help comes from the Lord,"
we cry aloud unto our God—
the One who hears the prayers
that sinners pray.

When Love appears, He brings us out
and sets our feet upon a rock,
for His way, we have "kept
and not declined" (Job 23:11).

All Things are Possible

Be not conformed to this world, but be transformed by
the renewing of your mind, so that you may prove what is
that good, and acceptable, and perfect, will of God.

—Romans 12:2

To be renewed in our minds, we must first devote ourselves
to God; only afterward may we "be blameless and harmless,
the sons of God, and without rebuke amid a crooked and
perverse nation" (Phil. 2:15). Though none can attain the heights or
the splendor of the Lord, the more transformed we become, the more
we experience the love of Christ, which passes all understanding.

Though she is but a worm,
she spins her silk cocoon and waits by faith
beneath the milky weed.

"Better is the end of a thing" (Eccles. 7:8),
she sings,
while spinning day and night
and night and day.

Once safe inside,
clothed in humility, she waits—
like one whose treasures are in heaven
where thieves cannot break-in.

Does she dream of monarch wings
that she may robe in a queenly gold
or royal red?

Or does she know no colored wings
dare to compare with those of faith
if she is one of His?

Perhaps the choicest wings await
those who believe—
and so, for her
"all things are possible" (Mark 9:23).

Lord,

Wherever we find ourselves today, teach us to live more prayerfully and more thankfully. When our enemies reproach us, even this we can bear, knowing You will turn away the things that we fear, for Your judgments are good.

Am I the Reason Why?

He stretches out the north over the empty place
and hangs the earth upon nothing.

—Job 26:7

From atop a high mountain, I stand on my tippy-toes and reach for the sky, pretending to touch the clouds that balance in the air. If I stand on the moon, I wonder, God, can I see the earth that "hangs upon nothing" (Job 26:7)?

Aside from being beautiful, a lily grows for no apparent reason. Does it know that "Solomon, in all his glory, was not arrayed like one of these" (Luke 12:27)? And how does a worm know to spin a cocoon and transform into a butterfly? Did You teach her so as she spins?

I have so many questions, God. If I stand and look from where You are, can I know "great things past finding out and wonders without number" (Job 9:10)? Will I see the trees that "clap their hands" (Isa. 55:12) and "hear the sea roar" (Ps. 98:7)? And God, how much do You love me?

What comforting words Your answer brings to me:

> Look past that "molten looking glass" (Job 37:18); look past the clouds that balance in the air and past the great beyond! Look farther than your eyes can see and past the east and west! Look farther than the north and south and then look farther still, and you will know how much I love you. Though I can do "great things past finding out and wonders without number" (Job 9:10), I can still hold on to you. But when you stand on your tippy-toes, I love you that much more.

Seeds that grow beneath the ground
and clouds that balance in the air—
snowflakes falling everywhere,
where do they all come from?

Herbs yielding seeds of their own kind,
and each fruit, its own seed inside—
incredible and wonderful,
where did they learn this from?

A painted worm comes out in June
and dizzily spins her cocoon.
Why does she hang there upside-down,
believing she can fly?

I've tried to figure it all out—
looked up and down and yet somehow
all things are past my finding out,
but still, I'd like to know.

Dear God,
I've searched both high and low,
from here and there and everywhere,
but most remarkable of all
is something I must know:

What earthly reason did You die?
Am I the reason why?

Lord,

You hung the sun high in the sky and the clouds that don't fall down. The birds all sing in harmony, and yet come from miles around! And You made me like one of these to fit right in Your plan; before I ever came to be, You held me in Your hand.

An Empty Chair

And the angel said unto him, Gird yourself, and bind
on your sandals. And so he did. And he said unto him,
Cast your garment about you and follow me.

—Acts 12:8

I had forgotten, until today, how knowing Jesus can bring solace
to a lonely heart. It is a drizzly day, and my heart has wandered
far from God.

The rain-washed window hinders my view of the cabins outside
and the colorful flowers lining the mountain road. Inside, it's lonely,
and the lights are dim, providing ample time for reflection.

I sip my coffee and think about my younger years when I shared
the gospel eagerly. Where did they go—those fruit-filled years? Now
I am old and all too familiar with the song of a lonesome cricket.

Beside You, Lord,
an empty chair waits for me.
Days of unspent moments in Your presence
take my place as I pass by.

Times of listening sit undone
as well as times for telling.
Beyond all measure
are the un-prayed prayers
You're waiting there to hear.

"With lovingkindness
have I drawn thee" (Jer. 31:3),
You say to me as I sit down.

O LORD of Hosts, God of Israel,
and He who dwells between the cherubim (Isa. 37:16),
how timeless is Your message unto me!

Left to myself, I'm blind in things of God—
lukewarm and dressed in filthy rags, I am.

Like gentle drops of rain from heaven,
Your words of love distill upon my heart
and lift my countenance.

What joy now fills my soul, as afterward,
I bind my sandals on and follow You.

Lord,

Find my heart Your home again that I may sup with You and You with me once more.

An Unexpected Swan of White

How precious are Your thoughts unto me, O God! How great
is the sum of them! If I should count them, they are more in
number than the sand: when I awake, I am still with You.

Psalm 139:17

When I am afraid, cause me to know the way wherein I
should walk; draw me closer, Lord, that I may know You
hear my anxious prayers.

"Seek my face," You answer, and my heart says back to You,
"Your face, LORD, will I seek" (Ps. 27:8). Like a feeble conie
running to a rocky place to feel secure, I run into Your arms where
I find peace and sense a feeling unexplained—like when I watch a
gosling sleep beneath its mother's wing.

Talking here with You, and You with me, no secret sin is hidden
from Your eyes, nor word upon my tongue that You don't know it
altogether. In this place of peace, precious are Your thoughts of me
and great beyond all measure!

Day and night, and night and day, You're at my side and know my
thoughts; "You know my sitting down and my uprising" (Ps. 139:2).
Forgetting my fragility, I jump for joy when standing from this
prayer that only we can have—like a child lets loose a kite to chase
a butterfly is this picture in itself that's ever-changing.

"The conies are a feeble folk
who make their houses in the rocks" (Pr. 30:26)
to feel secure.

Aware of their fragility
they run and hide in holes
and caves of Adullam.

But why are they afraid?
Perhaps a secret sin is whispering, *"Shh!"*
—soon to be found out!

Do we, like they who know not God,
run and hide in thorns and bushes
without hope?
If so, let's bow our heads and pray:

"Because O Lord,
You have redeemed my life,
I do believe."

"Boldly to Your throne of grace
I'll run, instead, where,
like an unexpected swan of white amid the geese,
You upend to find me
when I'm lost among the reeds."

As Long as I Have Breath

And Ruth the Moabitess said unto Naomi, Let me now go
to the field and glean ears of corn after him in whose sight I
shall find grace. And she said unto her, Go, my daughter.

—Ruth 2:2

E ven the sweetest dainties beyond the Jordan cannot compare
to the bread found in the Father's House; may we all be found
gleaning in this wealthiest of field.

Blessed assurance is abundant to all who do not eat the bread of
idleness. Those who glean in the Word of God, find handfuls of promises
from Him in whose omnipotent hand come all good things. "Bread shall
be given unto him, and his waters shall be sure" (Isa. 33:16).

Oh! Let us glean in the Shepherd's field
and speak out what we hear—
"Salvation is found in Christ alone!"

Will any stand for Him?
Such blesséd assurance to rest in One
whose thorn does keep us low.

Lastly, what I say is this:
"The harvest is plenteous,
but the laborers are few (Matt. 9:37).
As long as we have breath,
we must go out and glean the ears of corn."

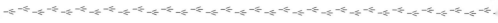

Lord,

There is not a more crucial moment in our lives than when we are encountered by You, for that moment sets in motion the rest of our lives, and afterward, we are never the same. "Behold, I make all things new," You say to us (Rev. 21:5), "and all that I have is yours" (Lk. 15:31). Thank You for granting us the right to live in Your grace and for the hope that is laid up for us in heaven.

As My Pages are Written

Let us lay aside every weight and the sin which does so easily
beset us, and let us run with patience the race that is set before
us, looking unto Jesus the author and finisher of our faith.

—Hebrews 12:1,2

While spending quiet moments with God in the early morning
hours, we hear the sound of footsteps on the pages of our
lives. In our arid wilderness, and with a steadied pen in
hand, the Word of God begins to write upon our hearts the things that
He would have us do. We have no need for pretty pictures on our walls
or painted faces to put on while we meet with Him each day.

His grace affects a change we've never known—
a gift from God, not of ourselves,
lest we should boast.

Within each chapter and each verse,
He makes a way that we might
be with Him in heavenly places.

While still artistry, we are,
He holds our covers in His hand,
and with one stroke, and with one word,
He writes, "Forgiven."

With wisdom, only He can give,
page-by-page His words reach out
to teach us in the way that we should go.

A scarlet thread between the leaves
bookmarks the pages He leaves out—
like the pain, He felt while suffering in our stead.

Line-by-line, and word for word,
He pens the answers that we need,
that we might share
a reason for our hope that lives inside.

"Give your life to Me," He writes,
"Confess your sins and be forgiven;
'Be born again' (Jn. 3:3)
that you may enter in."

Mere words cannot express
the newfound joy we feel inside,
as we let go of all the things we do not need.

Lord,

Find us not collecting dust, but lead us where we need to go, and we will follow page-by-page, unto the end.

Atop the Tip-Top of the World

The LORD gives wisdom: out of His mouth comes knowledge
and understanding. He lays up sound wisdom for the righteous:
He is a buckler to them that walk uprightly.

—Prov. 2:6-7

The Lord's almighty hand is sufficient to provide everything
we need. If we lack wisdom, He promises to provide it
"liberally and without reproach" (Jas. 1:5). Likewise, if we
are hungry, the "cattle on a thousand hills" (Ps. 50:10) are His to
give.

If only we would be like the Bereans, having our hearts fixed
on spiritual things and searching the scriptures daily. May we,
too, incline our ears to receive wisdom and apply our hearts to get
understanding, for "how much better it is to get wisdom than gold
and to get understanding rather than silver!" (Pr. 16:16).

My soul is happy down inside,
and no longer broken down.
I may never ask again,
"Why am I mourning and cast down?" (Ps. 43:2).

For I've inclined my ears to hear
the wisdom God gave Solomon
and asked for understanding,
"Lord, from where does wisdom come?"

Now she cries out in my streets,
and I hear understanding's voice,
"How much better to get wisdom,
finding her the better choice!"

My soul now plays the violin
atop the tip-top of the world.
It plays like one of His
whose cup is surely running over!

It dances on the mountains
like one raised who was bowed down,
and as one whom God gave wisdom
when the walls came falling down!

Lord,

"Where shall wisdom be found? And where is the place of understanding? A man knows not the price thereof; neither is it found in the land of the living. The depth says, 'It is not in me:' and the sea says, 'It is not with me'" (Job 28:12-14). Lord, from where does wisdom come? Where is the place of understanding?

Be Merciful, O God

For all the promises of God in Him are yes, and in
Him, Amen, unto the glory of God by us.
—2 Corinthians 1:20

Such refreshing words for all who thirst for the promises and
privileges of the gospel. Living in a world where troubles
abound on every side, they lift our hearts and remind us that
our help comes from God.

Many believers live as if God's promises aren't true. They forget
what He has done in days gone by and that He is the same yesterday,
today, and forever—the constant in our lives that never changes.

Like the children of Israel who laid down their instruments
and wept beside the rivers of Babylon, sometimes we, too, find
ourselves mourning over the state of our affairs. Though we belong
to Christ, and all things are ours through Him, we fail to remember
the spiritual riches of a true believer and, instead, hang "our harps
upon the willows" (Ps. 137:2). With our minds in a draught of the
gospel promises, we become like the dove that found no rest for her
foot, for apart from Christ Jesus, our Lord, there is no rest.

When my heart is overwhelmed,
and heaviness suspends this writer's quill,
dare I hang my harp upon the willow
and lodge in some vast wilderness?

Perhaps unto the hills, I'll run
where "mountains skipped like rams
and the little hills, like lambs" (Ps. 114:4).

Or perhaps not.

For from the hills,
salvation's hope is vanity (Jer. 3:23).

The mountains cannot speak:
"Come unto Me" (Matt. 11:28),
and God has set a boundary
around my endless searching (Ex.19:23).

While "the mountains quake
and the earth burns in His presence" (Nah. 1:5),
higher, still, I'll go
and look from heights of Mount Shénir.
And, there, I'll pray:
"Be merciful, O God."

After He has filled my quill,
I shall begin to write again:
"If I ascend to heaven,
You are there" (Ps. 139:8).

As billows calm across my soul,
I'll hear the mountains sing once more
and hear the trees begin to clap (Isa. 55:12)
as I'm led forth with peace.

Lord,

You are the solid rock on which we stand. Though the paths ahead may be uncertain, You assure us that we can have peace and joy when You are our strength. Help us live in harmony with one another and stay calm as we move forward, trusting in You.

Be Still and Know

Then He brought me and caused me to come to the brink
of the river. At the bank of the river were very many
trees on the one side and on the other. Then, He said unto
me: These waters issue out toward the east country and
go down into the valley, and into the sea: which being
brought forth into the sea, the waters shall be healed.

—Ezekiel 47:6-8

What comforting words to hear while walking hand-in-hand with the Lord—the One "touched with the feelings of our infirmities" (Heb. 4:15). Like gentle drops of water pouring down like rain, His Words of life distill upon our hearts and lift our countenance. In the stillness of the dawn, we lift a prayer to Him: "My voice shalt Thou hear in the morning" (Ps. 5:3).

"Be still, and know" (Ps. 46:10),
He answered while the daybreak,
as we sat together there beside the road.
Opening His Word, we read together:
"Blesséd be the name of the Lord" (Ps. 113:2).

"Be kind one to another," He imparted (Eph. 4:32),
as we turned and read His Words written in red.
"Have lowliness of mind" (Phil. 2:3)
for one another,
and forgive, as I've forgiven you,"
He said.

"A new commandment
I shall give you," He continued—
while giving us this day our daily bread.
"Love one another, as I have loved you" (Jn. 13:34),
and "follow after charity," He said (1 Cor. 14:1).

What sweeter supplication than, Dear Lord,
or better time to meet with Him each day?
Here we tell Him things He knows already,
and we learn of a "more excellent way" (1 Cor. 12:31).

Lord,

You are my God. Early will I seek You; my soul thirsts for You,
and "my flesh longs for You in a dry and thirsty land where no water
is" (Ps. 63:1).

Beautiful

And a certain man lame from his mother's womb was carried, whom they laid daily at the gate of the temple, which is called Beautiful, to ask alms of them that entered into the temple.

—Acts 3:2

Grief and sadness cause us to look to Jesus—the One who makes the blind see, the lame to walk, and the lepers clean. Step by step, as we climb the staircase of faith, we find ourselves safe in the arms of Jesus, resting in His wonderful grace that needs no earthly language.

Brought daily to the gate,
the lame man lay.
Crippled from his mother's womb,
he begs for alms from those who enter in.

"Beautiful," the gate is called (Acts 3:2)
and there, with simple words,
You lift him up in that ninth hour.

Like David, is he glad?
Does he exclaim:
"My feet shall stand within thy gates,
O Jerusalem?" (Ps. 122:2).

Sweet hour of prayer
there must have been for him.

Praise the Lord, for seed sewn there
to those assembled around like bees—
a reminder to us all,
"If I be lifted up …" (Jn. 12:32).

Best Friends

A man who has friends must show himself friendly: and
there is a friend who sticks closer than a brother.

—Proverbs 18:24

Brother, do you remember when we walked together down the
road? Barefoot, we walked, carrying fishing poles; the road
was graveled, but we didn't mind back then. We'd laugh or
throw a rock, and we stubbed our big toes now and then, but even
that seemed not to matter very much.

We built a treehouse way up high—a private hideout made with
stairs—and "swattin' flies" was something done in our spare time.

Those were the good-old-days for sure; the fish we caught were
all, "This big!"—a conversation between the two of us.

I've missed those days when strength was strong, and you and
me, well, we were friends—best friends—and that is matter-of-fact.
One day you turned to me and said, "There's nothing you and I can't
do." I knew right then I'd always have your back.

On the days when the sun refused to shine, our best-laid plans
were set aside, but did we care? If so, I don't remember when.

Those fun-filled days of yesteryear, if only we could have them
back—when fireflies could surely lead the way. With flashing jars
tightly in hand, "To that old house!" we'd holler out, and as if riding
painted horses, we would run. While there, we shook the walnut
trees once more.

As time went on, I went my way, and as life would have it, you
did too; this way and that, we traveled down the road.

Cassette tapes were the *newest thing*, especially the one you
gave to me; as I listened, you were many miles away. Christian songs
played front and back, and I rewound them; that's for sure because
they taught me how to walk the narrow way. Today, dear brother, my
life is changed because of you.

So,
when you think you've lived for naught,
I understand, for I've been there.
Life's barefoot rocky roads are everywhere.

Though that old house is gone by now
and miles between us, separate,
"where two or three are gathered" (Matt. 18:20)
in God's name, He is there.

So should you need to throw a rock,
know that we are here for you.

Why?

Because dear brother,
that's what best friends do.

Clandestine Charlatan

Your iniquities have separated between you and your God, and
your sins have hidden His face from you that He will not hear.

—Numbers 3:23

While resting on the mountainside, we watch a spider masterfully tooling its path of deception. Unsuspecting passersby will soon find themselves entangled in its glistening thread. Much like this, sin is sure to find us out (Num. 32:23).

Where are you, spider on the web?
What false professions do you weave
to foolish passersby?
Do those who marvel at your tooling,
notice not your barefaced lie?

Clandestine Charlatan,
"your lips have spoken lies" (Isa. 59:3).
Sir, I will call you Sin!

For there on a web of make-believe,
you masquerade on fragile lengths
of one consuming thread!

When your alluring web is spun,
each moment is uncertain
for unsuspecting guests,
for who can know the numbering of his days?

Long they stare at sinfulness,
idolatry, and vice,

until unaware, they are ensnared,
where you will "find them out" (Num. 32:23)!

Professing themselves wise,
they become fools
though Godly Wisdom tried to warn.

Excuse is left to plea when,
with a puff of wind, your cobweb's gone,
and you're exposed at last!

Lord,

Soon after rising from baptism, You were led by the Prince of Darkness to be tempted in the desert, but each time, Lord, You overcome! God forbid that we who are "dead to sin, live any longer therein" (Rom. 6:2).

Come up Hither

And I heard, as it were, the voice of a great multitude and as the voice of many waters, and as the voice of mighty thundering's, saying, Alleluia: for the Lord God omnipotent reigns.
—Revelation 19:6

I magine, if you will, looking beyond the top of a snow-capped mountain and seeing heaven's door opened; afterward, you hear the voice of a trumpet saying unto you, "Come up hither, and I will show you things which must come after" (Rev. 4:1). In much the same way, while exiled on Patmos island, "John saw the holy city, the new Jerusalem, coming down from God out of heaven prepared as a bride adorned for her husband" (Rev. 21:2).

Carried in the Spirit
amid sounds of thundering,
John hears the voice of many,
singing praises to the King.

The four-and-twenty elders
worship Jesus on the throne,
saying, "Amen; Alleluia" (Rev. 19:4)
to the One Who sits thereon.

Praise the Lord, you servants—
all who fear the great I AM.
Be glad, and come rejoicing,
to the marriage supper of the Lamb.

The Lamb is the burnt offering—
the One Who bled and died.

Beside Him, perfect and complete,
stands the Bride of Christ.

"The voice of a great multitude" (Rev. 19:6)
praise Him day and night.
While exchanging trials for mercies,
they receive a "robe of white" (Rev. 6:11)!

"Alleluia" (Rev. 19:6) they are singing
while lifting holy hands.
Alleluia to the King of Kings,
"the Lord God omnipotent reigns" (Rev. 19:6)!

Lord,

There is coming a day when You shall judge the secrets of all men according to the gospel. Happy are those who know they are justified on that great day.

Excelsior! Higher Still!

O my dove that is in the clefts of the rock, in the secret places of
the stairs, let me see your countenance, let me hear your voice.
—Song of Solomon 2:14

When life is good, we do not need a lion to stand watch
upon the mountain. But when the fiery darts of the
enemy make us afraid, how quickly we run into the
clefts of the rocks, crying, "Oh that I had wings like a dove! For then
I would fly away and be at rest!" (Ps. 55:6).

Do you sit near kindled fires
while the manna is falling free,
then as the flames get higher,
will far from them you flee?

Will you promptly
take the shield of faith
when the fiery darts are hot,
or will you firmly keep your distance
and exclaim, "I know Him not" (Lk. 22:57)?

Why does it take a certain maid,
who sees you where you are,
to say, "This one was with Him,"
as you deny Him by the fire (Lk. 22:56,57)?

O dove that hides in the clefts of the rock,
and secret places of the stairs,
God hears you chattering like a crane
when little foxes chase you there!

Know you not He quickly comes
when Satan lies in wait for you?
Like a lion watching from the mount
He will show Himself to you!

So place your confidence in Him
and let your voice exclaim:
"Excelsior! Higher Still!"
when you face a fiery flame.

Then as you walk amidst the blaze,
watch the shadows flee away,
as you trust that God is by your side
walking with you in the flame.

Except You See a Sign

Whosoever drinks of the water that I shall give him shall
never thirst; the water that I shall give him shall be in
him a well of water springing up into everlasting life.

—John 4:14

Looking down at the miry clay from which the Lord brought
us out, we tremble lest we should fall into it again; at the
same time, we rejoice to be privileged to walk with Him,
looking forward to heaven where there is no sin or depravity.

I introduced myself that day,
not knowing what that I should say,
when suddenly, an angel stood by me.

The angel said with certainty:
"Jesus came one afternoon
and sat beside a woman at this well."

As both of us looked down the well,
the angel said, in earnestness,
"He knew this woman
walked the longest mile."

Why has this angel come, I thought,
speaking as if to counsel me?
I asked the angel,
"What did Jesus say?"

"Though some would seek to condescend,
Jesus counseled her instead:
'Whosoever drinks of Me thirsts not again'" (Jn. 4:14).

"He knew the many things she'd done
and told her of the One to come,
saying to the woman, 'I Am He'" (Jn. 4:26).

The angel then looked up and said:
"I've come to say to you, like He,
'Except you see a sign, you won't believe'" (Jn. 4:48).

Lord,

We are all servants of sin until Your Spirit gives us new life. As we come into your presence, pour Your living water into our hearts that we may learn to love You more, for there is no spiritual life in us but what You place there.

Faithful and True

And I saw heaven opened, and behold a white horse, and
He that sat upon him was called Faithful and True.

—Revelation 19:11

Life is a journey, but it is not well sought after in the flesh; in fact, this kind of searching seldom leads down the narrow road. Only with the comforting promises of Jesus Christ and faith in His Word can we enjoy the path that leads to life.

Lord,

So many things to thank You for
as hereupon the mount
You bring good tidings.

All we are we owe to You,
the Greater Still, the living Word,
Majesty enthroned above,
and He who reigns forever!

A faithful friend, who can find?
You are that One
and boundless in Your love toward us.

Faithful and True, You are,
and always there amid the winds of change.

For Me to Live is Christ

For me to live is Christ, and to die is gain.
—Philippians 1:21

God's truth is eminent, yet how easily we find ourselves caught up in the lies of the enemy that threaten our peace. Whether we have a mountain-top experience or walk through a valley, we are enriched with the treasures of God. Regardless of fire or rain, the Lord is with us. "Through God, we shall do valiantly, for it is He that shall tread down our enemies" (Ps. 60:12).

"It is I, be not afraid" (Matt. 14:27),
You say to me,
when from the darkness to the Light, I run.

Light of the World,
I belong to You,
for I am in Your hand,
and forever, I shall be (Ps. 73:23).

"For me to live is Christ" (Phil. 1:21),
my heart declares;
"I in You, and You in me,
'perfect in One'" (Jn. 17:23).

What vast expanse can stand between
that I should send a messenger?
For You, O Lord, are in my selfsame house.

For Such a Time as This

You have turned for me my mourning into dancing: You
have put off my sackcloth and girded me with gladness.

—Psalm 30:11

While we sit beside a quiet mountain brook to pause and reflect, the presence of the Lord is with us. We watch as He sends the springs into the valleys to provide a drink for every beast of the field.

Unbelievers do not comprehend that it is the Lord who waters the hills from His chambers or that the earth is satisfied with the fruit of His hand; it is foolishness to them and hard to understand.

Such is the difference when speaking of death. Believers who lose a loved one pray with earnest expectation: "Lift me, O God, to Your strong-tower, that I may feel my heartache lose its power." Unbelievers cry instead: "If there were a God, He would not have let this happen!" For them, death only fans the flame of doubt about the existence of God.

What kind of heartbreak
brings one near to God?
Can any good come out of such a thing?

Behind barbed wires such as these,
grief sparks a wilderness of doubt,
but like a sparrow in His sight,
God sees us there.

Down on bended knee, we pray
to the One who holds all things in place:
life and death, cognizance,

and the rising of the tides—
things that only God Himself can know (Deut. 29:29).

When turning to His Words in red,
we read our penciled margins, too—
footnotes, perhaps,
for such a time as this.

Though we know not why flowers grow,
or why a Godly friend must die,
a promise is assured:

Those who close their eyes at night,
trusting God for the morning light,
are those who also die in Christ
and wake to find Him there.

Give Us This Day

I am the true vine, and my Father is the husbandman. Every branch
in Me that does not bear fruit He takes away: and every branch
that bears fruit, He purges, that it may bring forth more fruit.

—John 15:1

In the cool of the day, we hear the Lord walking in our gardens.
Will He find our vines full of ripened grapes and bearing fruit?
If we should stop and listen, perhaps we'd hear Him say: "The
harvest is plenteous, but the laborers are few" (Matt. 9:37).

The Word of God
—a piercing sword, indeed—
bears the Spirit of the Living God.

Quick and powerful it is,
dividing "joints and marrow" (Heb. 4:12).
No other sword is found
so sharply honed.

While feeding on His Bread,
no darkness shall prevail,
for those who acquiesce are taught to pray:
"Give us this day" (Matt. 6:11).

When rising to our feet,
we're like an embassy,
compelled as God's ambassadors
to bring forth fruit,
as our hearts, like Aaron's rod,
begin to bloom.

Great is Thy Faithfulness

I will sing of the mercies of the LORD forever: with my mouth
will I make known thy faithfulness to all generations.

—Psalm 89:1

O ne of the best remedies for sadness is to sing a song of
praise that brings glory to God. "Praise the Lord!" we sing,
"Praise the Lord! Let the earth hear His voice!"

Many of the psalms begin in lament and end in joy. Such is not
the case with Psalm 89. It poignantly begins in praise and ends in sad
redress—perhaps at a time, the house of David is woefully undone.

"I will sing of the mercies of the Lord forever," the penman of
scripture writes amid the sorrows of the day. How sweet His words
must be in the ear of the Savior, as they resound in the archways of
heaven.

Such is the song of the sparrow in the cold of winter. As darkness
lifts its mantle, even the choicest choir cannot out sing her joyful
sonnet, as she prays for the spring to come quickly.

Through joyful tears
and from the barest branch,
she whistles a melodious tune:
"Blessed assurance," the sparrow sings,
despite the winter's icy fetters.

Sweet fellowship indeed—
such blesséd hope to get alone with God.
While knocking resolute at mercy's door
she pleads with earnest compulsion.

Such believing expectation—
such faith in the efficacy of prayer!

What thing soever she desires,
believing, she receives,
and it is hers (Mk. 11:24).

As the frost of winter dissipates
into the sparkling dew of spring,
"Great is Thy faithfulness!" she sings,
while taking flight amidst His mercies, new.

Lord,

This is the day that You have made, I will rejoice and be glad in it (Ps. 118:24).

Hear From Wisdom

The Lord possessed me in the beginning of His way before His
works of old. I was set up from everlasting, from the beginning,
or ever the earth was. When there were no depths, I was brought
forth, and when there were no fountains abounding with water.
Before the mountains were settled, I was brought forth.

—Proverbs 8:22-23

W e open the Holy Bible and enter into a land of living
waters; there, we find the end of our searching: "Oh that
I knew where I might find Him!" (Job 23:3). Reading
further, we discover the knowledge of things both old and new,
declaring the right way we should live, and with each turning of
the page, a fresh supply of wisdom awaits to fertilize even the most
stagnant heart. More precious than rubies, she is, and all things
desired cannot compare.

The Lord brought wisdom forth
before the dust of the earth was born—
from everlasting and beginning,
and before all other works were formed.

He spoke, "Good Morning!" into time,
"Let there be light" (Gen. 1:3); she heard Him say.
As wisdom watched, the sun became.
And so it was on that first day.

She watched the stars stand tippy-toed
while God placed twinkles in their eyes.
She did not ask, "Does not one fail?"
the night He set them in the sky.

She knew the man up in the moon
illumined in a borrowed gown—
before he two-stepped high in praise,
or do-si'-do, God spun him around.

She saw the great leviathan
before God gave the sea decree,
and did not ask: "Are you the one
to swallow Jonah in the sea?"

So, hear from wisdom and be wise—
she leads in the "way of righteousness" (Pr. 8:20).
Blessed are they who seek for her,
for those who find her shall find life!

Lord,

Your hand is in everything, and You show Yourself faithful to
those who love You because that is who You are. Thank You, Lord.

Higher Still

When you are bidden, go and sit down in the lowest room;
that when he that bade you comes, he may say unto you:
Friend go up higher.

—Luke 14:10

I magine living continuously in that new experience of receiving Christ—that moment when you are first released from what the law can't do and into what the grace of God accomplished. What a delightful change the gospel affords those who come out of the darkness of law and into freedom in Christ. "Behold, I make all things new," Jesus said (Rev. 21:5), "and all that I have is yours" (Lk. 15:31).

When Jesus calls my name,
I take the lowest room in my unworthiness,
and there, in penitence,
my guilty soul does fall.

When after I have first believed
—amid the dust of sin left far behind—
Jesus stands on higher ground
and calls me, "Friend."

"Higher still," He says to me,
as I, in reverence, bow in my humility—
for all exalted flesh "shall be abased" (Lk. 14:11).

Seraphim, with wings of twain,
veil His face,
while at His feet, I stand as one of His.

Afterward,
there is joy in the presence of the angels of God
over one who has repented (Lk. 15:10).

Lord,

After we believe, we leave all childish things behind to put on Your armor in preparation for the battles of life. Create in us a new desire to love You more. Help us be consistent, so we may stay the course and proclaim Your Truths, for all "whose mind is stayed on You" (Isa. 26:3) have perfect peace. Thank You, Lord, for Your promise to care for all who call You Savior.

His Great Drops of Blood

Then Jonah prayed unto the LORD his God out of the fish's belly, and said, I cried by reason of my affliction unto the Lord, and He heard me; out of the belly of hell, cried I, and He heard my voice.

—Jonah 2:2

Remaining steadfast in the Word of God provides hope in times of trouble, enabling us to hold fast to our faith when life doesn't go as planned. Whether we dwell in the "uttermost parts of the sea" (Ps. 139:9) or flee to the highest mountain, the Lord is with us continually.

This truth became evident in Jonah's dark world after a great fish swallowed him in the sea. Feeling desperate and alone, he remembered the Words of the Lord and learned humility. When the Lord told the fish to vomit Jonah out on the dry land, one might rightly assume that the fish answered without hesitation: "Okay, Lord, I'm heading for the shore!"

> The waters compassed me about,
> and depths closed in,
> as weeds wrapped around my head (Jon. 2:5).

> Like Job, I stood before the Lord
> and heard Him say,
> "Can you bind the sweet influence of Plē'ə-dēz,
> or loose the bands of Orion?" (Job 38:31).

> With pride as my defense,
> I left the question far behind
> and sobbed instead,
> "What is man, that You are mindful,
> and the son of man, that You visit him?" (Ps. 8:4).

Absorbed in my self-pity,
I recalled the words of John:
"For God so loved the world" (Jn. 3:16).

Abruptly,
like the lamb that appeared to Isaac,
I fell upon my face
where brokenness surrendered pride.

I considered, as did Paul,
the sufferings of this present time
are not worthy to compare
with His "great drops of blood" (Lk. 22:44).

Lord,

When we choose to fight our own battles, often we find ourselves cast into a deeper sea of problems, but who is not stronger after bearing affliction, especially when You are with us? Show us when we are stubborn, and teach us to answer readily: "Here am I," no matter how high the water.

How Great Thou Art

When You said, 'Seek my face;' my heart said
unto You, 'Your face, LORD, will I seek.'
—Psalm 27:8

Memories of times spent climbing up the snow-clad mountains of Shénir and Tabor cause my heart to billow up and yearn for another ascent. Meanwhile, there is nothing like spending time beside a snowy foothill at autumn's end to seek the Lord. "Seek My Face" (Ps. 27:8), He says to me.

Have you seen the One
who *is* "the rose of Sharon" (Song of Sol. 2:1)?
His shoes, "I am not worthy to bear" (Matt. 3:11).
He *is* "the Lily of the Valley" (Song of Sol. 2:1).
If only I knew where I might find Him!

He withdrew into the wilderness this morning,
"rising up a great while before day" (Mk. 1:35).
To a solitary place, He went at first light,
and in that Holy place, my Savior prayed.

Perhaps He is atop the Mount of Herman,
talking there with Peter, James, and John—
the place whereby "His countenance was altered" (Lk. 9:29)
like "the skin of Moses' face" (Ex. 34:29)
when he came down.

Maybe I will find Him in the garden—
a place He can be found "in the cool of the day" (Gen. 3:8).
How I long to tell Him that I love Him;
"How Great Thou Art,"
I'll sing along the way.

"Saw you Him whom my soul loves?" (Song 3:3).
Yes! Siméon once held Him in his arms (Lk. 2:28).
He has promised if I seek Him, I shall find Him,
but only if I search "with all my heart" (Jer. 29:13).

Lord,

You are our sure confidence, keeping our foot from being taken. Establish our comings and goings, and cause us to walk by the rivers of waters in a straightway.

I Am Joshua, the Son of Nun

Moses, my servant, is dead; now therefore arise, go over
this Jordan, you, and all these people, unto the land which
I do give to them, even to the children of Israel.

—Joshua 1:2

A day of rejoicing in the Lord is a day to be desired. Sitting beside Joshua and listening to him tell of God's goodness was, perhaps, one of those days. However, after his sermon, Joshua died, being one hundred and ten years old (Josh. 24:29).

One might question why Joshua's story has such a sudden ending, but God is faithful to the end, for shortly after crossing over the Jordan, Joshua stepped into heaven to be with the Lord—the promised land for all who believe.

I am Joshua, "the son of Nun" (Josh. 17:4),
and I have now waxed old.
Behold, this day I go the way
that all the earth must go.

When I cross the Jordan,
without blemish, I will be,
for I have kept "the charge of keeping" (Num. 3:38),
as the Lord commanded me.

In the land of my possession
sanctified and made complete,
the first is last, and the last is first—
spot or wrinkle, there won't be.

There, I'll never say again:
"What a wretched man I am!" (Rom. 7:24)
after crossing over the Jordon
into the Promised Land.

Take heed, henceforth, unto yourselves,
to love the Lord your God;
taste the milk and honey,
and observe what God has done.

Divide the riches in your tents
and recover your own lot;
"One man of you
shall chase a thousand" (Josh. 23:10),
and the Lord shall be your God.

Delight in Him unto the end
while you live in Canaan land—
until the day we meet again
in the New Jerusalem!

Lord,

The sounds of heaven ring as we read: "Come, blessed of my Father, and inherit the kingdom prepared for you" —Mt. 25:34. Even so, Lord, take us to that holy place beyond Amana, and that place beyond the peaks of Shénir and Tabor where, like Joshua, we may forever bask in Your everlasting arms. Thank You for the eternal happiness that awaits those who die in Christ.

I Am the Lord

I am Alpha and Omega, the beginning, and the
ending, says the Lord, which is, and which was,
and which is to come, the Almighty.

Revelation 1:8

I magine, if you will, finding a quiet place on the mountain and
opening a letter penned to you from the heart of someone dear:
"Beloved," it reads, "Where shall I begin?" While sitting on a
comfortable rock, you open the Word of God and find such a letter;
"In the beginning," you read.

Who made a "way in the wilderness" (Isa. 43:19),
and who parted the sea (Isa. 43:16)?
Who said to Moses, "I AM THAT I AM" (Ex. 3:14),
and who said, "Come unto Me" (Matt. 11:28)?

Who wrote upon your heart of flesh,
"not with ink or tables of stone" (2 Cor. 3:3)?
And who said to you,
"Won't you come and dine?" (Jn. 21:12).
Know you not that it was the Lord?

See how "the rivers run into the sea,
and yet the sea is not full" (Eccl. 1:7)!
And unto the place from where rivers come,
again, they return once more!

Who set the earth spinning 'round like a ball
and the moon to stand still in the air?
Who split the waters of the "great-big wide"
with a "strong east wind" (Ex. 14:21) blowing there?

Know you not, it was the Lord
seated high upon His throne—
the "Alpha and Omega,"
and He who "is to come" (Rev. 1:8)?

Yes! It is God "who called the earth
from the rising of the sun" (Ps. 50:1),
and "before the day was" (Isa. 43:13),
He is there,
"unto the going down thereof" (Ps. 50:1).

Lord,

Who is like You, O God? You are the Creator, who made the heavens and the earth, and by Your hand, "all things consist" (Col. 1:17). Blesséd is Your name, from this time forth and forever.

I Belong to You, O God

And He that sat upon the throne said, Behold, I
make all things new. And He said unto me, Write:
for these words are true and faithful.

—Revelation 21:5

What an earnest call to pause and consider these words
of the Lord; indeed, it is He who sits on the throne and
does a work in us that we cannot do—transforming us so
that we hardly know ourselves. "Change my heart, O God," we pray.

God provides all things that pertain to life and godliness through
the knowledge of His son, Jesus Christ. In His Word, we find
"exceeding great and precious promises: that by these, we might
be partakers of the divine nature" (2 Pet. 1:4). Let us be diligent in
giving full adoration to Him Who has called us "out of darkness into
His marvelous light" (1 Pet. 2:9).

The day is Yours,
and the night You have ordained;
the summer and the winter,
You have made (Ps. 74:16-17).

Even after I have slept,
I wake refreshed because of Thee.
Lord, I awake,
for You have sustained me (Ps. 3:5).

"For me to live is Christ," I sing (Phil. 1:21),
while early shadows flee away.
"And when I die,
I've everything to gain!" (Phil. 1:21).

Though in a "strait between the two" (Phil. 1:22-23),
I belong to You, O God—
my flesh is weak,
but my spirit is "renewed" (Eph. 4:23).

While I walk with You today,
I have Your Word to light my way
as I profess,
"For me to live is Christ" (Phil. 1:20).

That where I go, Lord, You shall lead;
when I sleep, Lord, You shall keep,
and when I wake,
Your Word shall speak to me (Prov. 6:22).

I Go a Fishing

Simon Peter said to them, I go a fishing. They say unto him,
We shall go with you. They went forth and entered into a
ship immediately, and that night they caught nothing.

—John 21:3

T o hunger for the Bread of Life is to hunger for the Lord Jesus
Christ, who promises that our bread shall be given to us, and
our "waters shall be sure" (Isa. 33:16).

In the Bible, we read stories of Jesus seated on a high mountain
or walking beside the sea, talking to His disciples. One such account
describes Him calling out to them from the shore of Galilee, asking:
"Children, have you any meat?" (Jn. 21:5).

O Tiberias,
"the Sea of Galilee" (Jn. 6:1), you are,
and there, "I go a fishing" (Jn. 21:3).
But when I cast my net,
the night hour brings me naught!

When morning comes,
Jesus stands upon your shore,
but I know not that it is He (John 21:4),
when "Cast again," He says.

O Sea of Galilee,
like a shepherd, feeding flocks by night,
such reward He brings to me!
When afterward, I cast again,
in swim one hundred fifty-three (Jn. 21:11)!

You ask, O sea,
"Is there a table in the wilderness?" (Ps. 78:19),
for there, upon your shore,
Jesus breaks bread (Jn. 21:13).

Tiberias,
so many other things He did,
"the world itself could not contain
the books that should be written" (Jn. 21:25).

Lord,

If You should ask: "Do you love Me," I will reply, "Yes, Lord; You know that I love You" (Jn. 21:15). If You should ask me again, I will answer the same, "Yes, Lord; You know that I love You" (Jn. 21:16). I will follow You all the days of my life.

I Prayed for Rain

Show me a token for good; that they who hate
me may see it, and be ashamed: because You,
Lord, have helped me and comforted me.

—Psalm 86:17

We owe our very existence to God and are dependent on Him for all things; even our faith does not come from ourselves but is wrought in us by God.

We would not have looked to the cross and recognized our need for Christ had it not been for His first removing the veil from our eyes. May we all place our trust in Him with an expectation that cannot be shaken, believing that He anticipates our prayers before we ask and that He will give us what is best out of the abundance of His goodness.

I climbed up to the plateau of Mount Carmel,
where all night long, I prayed unto the Lord.

I cast myself "upon the earth" (1 Kgs. 18:42:42)
and bowed my face between my knees—
but *nothing* was the answer that I heard.

My prayers went up again and again,
as if to beg from Jacob's rung,
then seven more times, I prayed for rain.

As I waited there in prayer,
I saw a wind, a quake, and fire,
but no rain, and neither was He there.

Holding on with childlike faith,
I prayed, "Lord, help my unbelief,
and show me a small token for my good" (Ps. 86:17).

As I stood atop the mount,
"a little cloud rose from the sea" (1Kgs. 42-44),
and from the hand of God,
a "great rain" (1 Kings 42:45)
fell on me.

Lord,

We can do nothing apart from You; even our faith is a gift from You. Thank You for providing salvation to us through Your Son, Jesus Christ, and for Your Holy Spirit that works in us "both to will and to do of Your good pleasure" (Phil. 2:13).

If I am Lifted Up

The flood was forty days upon the earth, and the waters
increased, and bare up the ark, and it was lifted above the earth.
—Genesis 7:17

The Lord made "His sun to rise on the evil and the good"
(Matt. 5:45). Today, we look up and see a little cloud over the
mountain and know that soon the rain will fall on both "the
just and on the unjust" (Matt. 4:45). "Be exalted, O God, above the
heavens; let Your glory be above all the earth" (Ps.57:5), the psalmist
writes. May this be our prayer, too, as we rise early and prepare our
hearts to say unto the world: "So says the Lord" (Ex. 8:20).

O little cloud with a heavy heart,
why are you downcast?
Will you sail away before your work is done?

But are not clouds without the rain
like those who boast (Pr. 25:14)?
And unless waves bare up the ark,
are "eight souls" (1 Pet. 3:20) saved?

O darkened cloud up in the sky,
what if "I am lifted up" (Jn. 12:32)
had not concluded:
"I will draw all men to Me" (Jn. 12:32)?

Hear from Solomon:
"A spring shut up; a fountain sealed" (Song 4:12)
is not what God intends for you to be.

When the skies are overcast,
and rainy days are planned for you,
know it is God who sends
the "rain upon the earth" (1 Kings 18:1).

O cloud,
He brings you over the earth
so that His promise is fulfilled:
"My bow shall be seen in the cloud" (Gen. 9:14).

Lord,

A day to rejoice in the things You have made is a day to be desired. Take possession of our hearts, so our mourning is turned to dancing, our mouths are "filled with laughter, and our tongue with singing" (Ps. 126:2).

Is it Left Only in White?

And it shall come to pass, that before they call, I will
answer; and while they are yet speaking, I will hear.

—Isaiah 65:24

David writes: "Blessed be God who has not turned away my
prayers, nor His mercy from me" (Ps. 66:20). It is good to
be reminded of this truth as we commune with God upon
the high mountain.

We often read books about God yet fail to look up from the
written lines and speak to Him face to face. Like casting nets and
expecting a draught, great and mighty things remain for us behind
the prayers God wants to hear, but nothing keeps His listening
ear from hearing all our prayers except our lack of lifting them
to Him.

We read, and read again,
every jot and every tittle about God
and marvel at the love He has for us,
but do we pray?
Or do we leave our prayers in white
between the lines where no eyes go?

If our stumbling eyes, perchance,
should wander from the lines,
will long we stay?

In these white space moments,
are our words as bountiful to God
as on the written line,
or will we find ourselves in foreign land?

How much we miss when
reading books *about* the Lord,
we fail to meet Him face-to-face.

Better poetry between the lines
speaks volumes, still,
waiting perhaps, to tell us
what no pen could ever write.

To go into our closets with the Lord
and feel our burdens lifted as we pray,
is a story written without lines
that every soul should read.

Lord,

There is no better place than here in prayer, and it is a shame we do not utilize its benefits more often. May our prayers "be set forth before You as incense, and the lifting of our hands as the evening sacrifice" (Ps. 141:2), and may this lead us to more earnest prayer.

Is There Not a Cause?

And David said, What have I now done? Is there not a cause?
—1 Samuel 17:29

What unparalleled bravery for David to challenge a Philistine champion like Goliath. A remarkable victory is won with just a sling and a stone. Except for God's provision of "five smooth stones out of the brook" (1 Sam. 17:40), David relied solely on his faith in God. "This day, the LORD will deliver you into my hand" (1 Sam. 17:46), he said to the giant, "and all this assembly shall know that the Lord saves not with a sword and spear: for the battle is the LORD's, and He will give you into my hand" (1 Sam. 17:47).

"Is there not a cause?" (1 Sam. 17:29),
young David asks,
when Goliath draws near with his sword.
"You come to me with a sword, and a spear,
but I come in the name of the Lord" (1 Sam. 17:45)!

In his strength alone and in want of fame,
the giant walks into the field;
closer to David, the Philistine came
with a man in front as a shield.

Young David says,
while holding a sling
and five smooth stones in his bag,
"This day, the Lord will fight for me
and deliver you into my hand" (1 Sam. 17:46).

Now, most of us know Goliath's fate
from the truth, the Bible tells.
The reason being "that the earth may know
there is a God in Isráel" (1 Sam. 17:46).

Just like the son of an Ephrathite
slew Goliath with a stone,
no problem we face is too big for us,
for the battle belongs to the Lord!

Lay your giant's at His feet,
so the Lord may fight for thee,
then say like Paul,
"From the paw of the lion,
the Lord delivered me" (1 Sam. 17:37)!

It's but a Chariot!

Fear not, for I am with you; be not dismayed, for I am your God.
—Isaiah 41:10

The storms of life bring sleepless nights to those who do not know the Lord; they are "like a wave of the sea driven with the wind and tossed" (Jas. 1:6). Those whose hearts are prepared beforehand know that it is God who "makes the storm a calm so that the waves thereof are still" (Ps. 107:29), and because they trust in the Lord, He will keep them "in perfect peace" (Isa. 26:3).

It is faithlessness to be afraid
if God shall go before "a lively hope" (1 Pet. 1:3).

Dear child of God,
"be not dismayed" (Isa. 41:10),
for though the clouds are thick,
the Lord is "on the top of the mount" (Ex. 19:20)
and in the "midst of the fire" (Deut. 4:33)!

Who is this pharaoh of your fears,
that strives to overtake you in the *Sea of Red*,
if you are one of His?

Dear Thomas, look again!
It's but a chariot—
an opportunity to trust the Lord, instead.
He has "overcome the world" (Jn. 16:33)
that we might live in Him whose
blood is *redder* still.

Lord,

Who is like You, O God? Your doctrine drops as the rain; Your speech distills as the dew, as the small rain upon the tender herb, and as the showers upon the grass (Deut. 32:2). It is You, Lord, who spoke peace to the tides and "triumphed gloriously: the horse and his rider You have thrown into the sea" (Ex. 15:1).

Jesus Loves Me, This, I Know

It is a fearful thing to fall into the hands of the living God.
—Hebrews 10:31

When faithlessness surrounds us like the shadows, and sparks fly upward in the darkest rooms, there is no greater calm than to hear the Lord say, "Fear not, for I am with you; be not dismayed, for I am your God" (Isa.41:10).

"Woe is me,
that I sojourn in Meshech
with the likes of hateful men" (Ps. 120:5,6).
"I dwell in the tents of Kadar" (Psa. 120:5),
Lord, and foolish, I have been.

Because of my defiance,
—like a blight upon the wood—
can You have compassion
on one who is not good?

"What son is he," You say to me,
"whom the Father chastens not?" (Heb. 12:7).
"It is a fearful thing to fall
into the hands of the living God" (Heb.10:31).

"My feet are almost gone," O Lord,
and "my steps have well-nigh slipped" (Ps. 73:2).
"Guide me with Your counsel" (Ps. 73:24)
and keep me in Your grip.

Keep my feet from falling, Lord;
so it is well down in my soul.
Lift my voice that I might sing:
"Jesus loves me, this, I know!"

Hear me calling: "Abba! Father!"
when like a sheep, I go astray,
and when You come to find me,
"This, I know," Lord, I will say.

Lord,

You knew me in the wilderness, "in the land of great drought" (Hosea 13:5). Though I was loathsome and lost in sin, still, You chose me in my fallen state. Most gracious Lord, You are my God, and there is none besides Thee.

Joy for Mourning

The Spirit of the Lord God is upon me to give unto them beauty
for ashes, the oil of joy for mourning, and the garment of praise
for the spirit of heaviness; that they might be called trees of
righteousness, the planting of the LORD, that He might be glorified.
—Isaiah 61:3

On this day of summer's end, look up to the heavens and say
unto the Lord: "You are my God, and I will praise You: You
are my God, I will exalt You. This is the day which the Lord
has made; I will rejoice and be glad in it" (Ps. 118:24, 28).

Weeping may endure for a night,
but the morning light brings with it —joy!
"Beauty for ashes" (Isa. 61:3)
I exchange.

I hear You answer, after:
"Make this valley ready for the waters,
though wind, nor rain,
you shall not see" (2 Kings 3:16,17).
And so, I do.

With full assurance, afterward, I wait;
though showers ne'er there be,
I watch as living waters fill my brook
just as You said.

A look from the top of Shénir Mountain
finds my "wilderness like Eden,
and my desert like the garden of the LORD" (Isa. 51:3),
and glad, I am.

Knock, Knock, Knock

The LORD looks from heaven; He beholds all the sons of men.
—Psalm 33:13

As I lower down my sail and waves come crashing down inside my heart, I have no words to say. The Lord stoops down with His inclining ear, but still, my words won't come. Lost inside my sorrows, I turn the light out in the room.

Feelings of defeat make Him wait outside my door as I think about tomorrow, trying to peek into a place I cannot see. Darkness fills the room, and I pretend that I can see a perfect world.

Looking all around, here and there, I search to find where best-laid plans are hiding. Shall I fetch my knowledge from afar? "Where is God, my Maker, who gives songs in the night?" (Job 35:10). Lost in my self-pity, I cry myself to sleep and fall to pieces.

There comes a knocking at my door, but I'm too full of sleep to rise. If I should lift my eyes, perhaps I'll see the Lord—like a night-light—watching over me. Still, I have no words to say.

Knock, knock, knock, I hear again. Compelled to understand, I turn and speak into the night: "What an earnest matter concerns You, especially of me?" With swords around my heart, I lay there guarded, pretending that He cannot understand. Before I turn again to seek those things I cannot find, He whispers in my ear: "Consider not the things of old" (Isa.43:18). "Behold, I do a new thing; will you not know?" (Isa. 43:19). In brokenness, I rise to hear the voice of my Redeemer: "Put on your garment and follow Me" (Matt. 11:29). When I obey, the heartstrings of my unstrung harp begin again to play a song of hope as I look up from Mount Shénir that I might see Him step out in the clouds—an expected end for all who wait for Him (Jer. 29:11).

Defeat would make You wait
outside my heart
as though You were a stranger, when,
knock, knock, knock, I hear.

Too full of sleep, I am, to rise;
what an earnest matter concerns You,
especially of me?

Awake and rise
from your unrest,
for He, Who is from Heaven,
stoops to you with His inclining ear!

Be mindful, too, defeated one:
though swords devour roundabout,
the Pharaoh of your fears is but a noise,
and past his time appointed (Jer. 46:17).

Awake, awake,
and look by faith from heights of Mount Shénir.
If you see nothing, still,
"go seven times again" (1 Kgs. 18:43)!

As you pray with fervent hope,
search your heart that all is good,
then pray, and pray again,
until you see a cloud arise!
—a token sign
that "fervent prayer avails" (Jas. 5:16).

Let Me Give of These

O God, You have taught me from my youth: and
hitherto have I declared Your wondrous works.

—Psalm 71:17

While speaking to the Lord "with the harp, and the voice of a Psalm" (Ps. 98:5), David writes: "I will praise You, O God, among the people: and I will sing praises unto You among the nations" (Ps. 108:3). It is good to exalt the Lord, openly, taking all occasion to speak well of Him, so that others may be affected by His goodness.

Spending time in the presence of the Lord makes us spiritually healthy and happy. He is the reason for the melody in our hearts and the smiles on our faces, and the more time we spend with Him, the happier we are. "I will bless the Lord at all times," the Psalmist declares, "His praise shall continually be in my mouth" (Ps. 34:1).

Lord,
A giver of grace, I want to be,
and that, without measure.

Draw me near to You,
and find me willing to share
with both my hands
the choicest gifts You've given me:

"Ways of pleasantness" (Prov. 3:17)
in knowing You,
and paths of peace like no other—
Your Words of Life,
and treasures like these, O God.

Meekness that makes my heart to live
and the joy I feel while feasting in Your blessedness.
Yes, Lord, let me give of these.

Impart in me
Your words of wisdom,
spreading health to all
who want of Your good pleasure.

Go before me in all things,
and I will follow—
holding fast to that which I have learned.

Most of all,
fill my heart with charity,
that I may share with all I meet
the spiritual blessings You have given me.

My Soul Does Magnify the Lord!

He that dwells in the secret place of the Most High
shall abide under the shadow of the Almighty.

—Psalm 91:1

Those who dwell in the secret place of the Highest have a beautiful work of grace begun in their souls, for God has opened their understanding that they may "sup with Him and He with them" (Rev. 3:20). "My heart is inditing a goodly matter," the psalmist writes, and "my tongue is the pen of a ready writer" (Ps. 45:1). Like this penman of scripture, those who commit their hearts to the Lord find peace, and demonstrate with outward expression, the beautiful things God is doing in their lives.

When I write, I find You there—
the Solace of my soul.
And where You are, all hope abounds.

With quill in hand, I speak to You,
O God of heaven and the earth—
mindful, You are all, and I am naught.

"My soul does magnify the Lord" (Lk. 1:46) I cry,
though not from high upon a hill,
but from my heart
where You, alone, can hear.

With feathered quill pressed to the page,
my heart pours out with steadied ink;
before I write, You know what I will say.

Despondency gives up
like fruitless blossoms on a tree when,
"Higher, still,"
You say unto my soul.

Raptured in Your love, I pen:
"Lead me to the Rock" (Ps. 61:2),
that secret place "higher than I" (Ps. 61:2),
O, God.

The place You "make me to lie down;
that place You lead me, Lord, beside" (Ps. 23:2)
—that special place where pastures are green
and waters are still.

My Unstrung Harp

By the rivers of Babylon, we sat down; we
wept when we remembered Zion.

—Psalm 137:2

Soothing notes perfume the air as David plays his harp despite his sorrows. "It is good to give thanks unto You, Lord," he writes, "and to sing praises to Your Name" (Ps. 92:1). In heaven, we, too, might play "an instrument of ten strings, and upon the psaltery and the harp with a solemn sound" (Ps. 92:3).

When I hide
like a hunted partridge on the mount
and hang my unstrung harp upon the willows,
You know my wanderings.

Like a shepherd seeks a long-lost sheep,
You search with breathless mercy
for such a one as me.

God of my salvation,
shield me from the guilt of sin,
that I hear not the cry:
"Crucify Him, crucify Him" (Lk. 23:21)!

Help me not to waver, Lord,
for day and night temptations taunt,
and like waves of the sea,
I'm driven by the wind and tossed.

I ask in faith, believing, Lord,
that I may play again upon my harp
the songs of Your great faithfulness.

May all my sonnets be
"God is my Salvation,"
for in this truth,
no melancholy note dares tarry around
when You are for me.

Cover me with a "garment of praise" (Isa. 61:3)
that I may tune my harp despite myself
and sing the song of David:
"I will love Thee, O Lord, my strength" (Ps. 18:1).

Lord,

"When we pass through the waters, You will be with us, and through the rivers, they shall not overflow us: when we walk through the fire, we shalt not be burned; neither shall the flame kindle upon us (Isa. 43:2). Thank You for this cup of grace, bringing joy to all who drink thereof.

No Hay Nadie Como Tú

But Jesus said, Suffer the little children, and forbid them
not to come unto me: for such is the kingdom of heaven.

—Matthew 19:14

David enjoyed shepherding his young lambs and was known
as the "sweet psalmist of Israel" (2 Sam. 23:1). "Come, dear
children," he said, "Hearken unto me, and I will teach you
the fear of the Lord" (Ps. 34:11). As one by one, the children came
to David, he taught them: "Children obey your parents in the Lord:
for this is right. Honor your father and mother, which is the first
commandment with promise; that it may be well with you, and you
may live long on the earth" (Eph. 6:1).

They listened as he played his harp,
and they watched him bend the bow,
"Harken unto me" (Ps. 34:11), he said,
as he taught them to "fear the Lord" (Ps. 34:11).

"Keep your tongue from evil
and your lips from speaking lies" (Ps. 34:13),
"Obey your parents in the Lord,
for this is right" (Eph. 6:11),
he said.

Red and yellow, black, and white
—diverse in tongue and nation, too—
came the little children, Lord,
as he bid them unto You.

See them bow down on their knees,
singing a simple little tune,
"Jesus loves me, this I know,
no hay nadie como Tú" (There is none like You)

Hear them sing in one accord,
"For the Bible tells me so,"
while others echo the refrain,
"Want de Bijbel, verteltz het zo!"

Lord,

We say unto You, "This I know, and this I don't—yet will I trust." Exercise Your mighty power in us to obey Your Word and to share the story of Your love from Genesis to Revelation. As people from every tribe, tongue, and nation hear of Your salvation, may their eyes be opened to understand the scriptures, so they, too, may proclaim: "There is none like You!"

On Bended Knee

I will remember my covenant between Me and you
and every living creature of all flesh, and the waters
shall no more become a flood to destroy all flesh.
—Genesis 9:15

How does a Christian live happily, or live at all, if he has not the assurance that his life is in Christ? If it were not for the Lord supplying fresh oil out of the abundance of His mercy and grace, soon our lamps would burn out, and without the promise that Jesus will complete what He has begun, there would be no hope of reaching Heaven.

It is reassuring to know that the Lord Jesus keeps "that which we have committed unto Him" (2 Tim. 1:12). Knowing that he hides us "under the shadow of His wings" (Ps. 17:8), we should never be without joy or singing, attending our steps, for the Lord has not forgotten us, and He keeps His promises.

If colors in the bow could speak,
perhaps we would hear the words of God:
"The waters shall no more
become a flood" (Gen. 9:15)
—the spoken memorandum
found in rainbows up above.

God's promise in the rainbow is not seen
unless His spoken words reflect the *Son*—
like the calmness of the sea, unknown,
until Jesus walked thereon.

You who are heavy-laden come
on bended knee—
the place a contrite heart
God can't despise.

In Christ alone,
no sharpened arrow can prevail
against a broken bow—
another promise kept in darkened skies.

Lord,

Clutched inside my heart is all I have—a prayer that I'm in need to pray. Find me at Your feet, and let Your strength take full command. Hear my silenced song that has wandered far from me— my *Hosanna to the Greater Still* that I can't find.

On the Old Rugged Cross

He was wounded for our transgressions; He was bruised
for our iniquities, and by His stripes, we are healed.

—Isaiah 53:5

T he kind of love the world had never known descended from heaven and died a death so undeserved. The nails that hung Him on the cross would feel no pain but His, while those in armor hung Him there to die.

Who was guilty of such crimes that Majesty enthroned above should come to earth and "give His life" (Mt. 20:28)? Those who nailed Him on the cross knew He was "the Son of God" (Mk. 15:39) and the Savior of the world.

On the soldiers hammered until death, that should have fallen on the sinner, fell on Christ. While some He came to save "esteemed Him not" (Isa. 53:3), those who loved Him knew that He who hung between the thieves cleared the way to heaven for us all. "Bruised for our iniquities" (Isa. 53:5), the people saw their punishment for sin upon the Savior of the world.

While angels watched from heaven as the Savior died, perhaps the six-winged seraphim refused to fly—sorrowed at the sight of Jesus bearing the sins of man. The people standing near could surely hear their never-ending cries: "Holy, holy, holy, is the Lord" (Isa. 6:3)!

We, too, were objects of His wrath, for human judgment, brought the Lord "to give His life a ransom" (Matt. 20:28) for us all. Because the message of the cross reminds us of the suffering Jesus laid upon Himself, "how shall we, who are dead to sin, live any longer therein?" (Rom. 6:2).

God sent
Jesus Loves Me
to a world
that did not care.

"This I know,"
was in the hearts
of those who hung Him there.

On The Old Rugged Cross
as they nailed His **Majesty**,
He opened
up their eyes,
for they were blind,
but now they see

Crying,
Holy, Holy, Holy,
and
Worthy Is the Lamb
they now
Gather at the River
singing:
Just as I Am.

Lord,

How can we thank You beyond our best or lift our hands in praise beyond their reach? Even if it were possible, better, and higher would not be enough. Thank You, Lord, for Your gift of Salvation and for loving us with an everlasting love.

One More Moment

To everything, there is a season
and a time to every purpose under the heaven.
—Ecclesiastes 3:1

S uch a timely message as we enter a new season—a time to cast off things we do not need, and "sing unto the LORD a new song" (Ps. 96:1). Though the uncertainties of each new day descend upon us like falling leaves, each moment is a gift from God, and fresh mercies such as these deserve new songs.

In the course of nature, every season has its turning divinely appointed by God. As the days surrender to the evening, and the sun lowers its shade, the moon stands still in its time. Sleep awhile, and we find ourselves waking again to His mercies that are "new every morning" (Lam. 3:23).

Such is the difference between children and men. While chasing fireflies, they reach out into the blinking darkness, having no thought for their lives "what they shall eat, or what they shall drink" (Matt. 6:25). When they are old, they put away childish things: "I have been young, and now I am old" (Ps. 37:23), the psalmist writes.

Only the Creator knows the numbering of our days, appointing a boundary unto us that we cannot pass. Neither can we comprehend the times or seasons set up by His power. When "the branch is yet tender, and putting forth leaves" (Matt. 24:32), only then do we know that summer is near.

God is the only constant in our lives. Prayers never go out of season, and even the most blistered soul can find solace in Him, for He is "ready to forgive and plenteous in mercy to all who call upon His name" (Ps. 86:5).

Lord,

If You should add one more moment to our lives, may it be like rain from heaven, bringing us "fruitful seasons, and filling our hearts with gladness" (Acts 14:17).

Return to Me

Even from the days of your fathers, you are gone away
from my ordinances and have not kept them. Return unto
Me, and I will return unto you, says the Lord of hosts.
—Malachi 3:7

Because of You, O God, I lack no good thing, yet my wayward heart has drifted far from You. Oppressed, I fly with a broken wing wearied from my wandering. Hear me calling, Lord, as I come home, that You might make my mountain strong again.

Forgive me, God, and heal my contrite heart, while through the blurry lines of distance, I fly homeward—hungry for the Bread of Life. Whatsoever things are right, whatsoever things are honest, and pure and lovely things—how I hunger for these things, O God. Hear my supplications, and bid my anxious thoughts, "Depart!"

Joy comes in the morning, as You mend my broken wing and draw me closer. While shadows flee, Your peace, that knows no measure, leads me by Your light of grace, that I may see Your Holy Hill through brightening skies. Though way too far, I've flown, Your mercies lead me safely home, for You have purchased me at such great price.

Breaths of wind lift me higher, still, where I can feel Your guiding hand beneath my wings. While I hold on to faith I cannot see, guard my unbelief with Your eyes that never sleep. Hear me calling: "Jesus! Master!" Oh how sweet the name that never fails my heart.

I hear the sound of angel's wings as nearer, Lord, I come to You. Thankful for the calm after the storm, and riding now on silver clouds, Your Mercy hastens to my side, where the sound of joy in heaven rings, as chains of sin release (Lk. 15:10).

She flew as if to soar
through endless boundaries;
blindly she ignored the floods ahead.
All the while wearied from her wanderings,
she hungered for her Master's daily bread.

Greater distance blurred the lines between them
as farther still, she left the ark behind.
Longing for her long-lost habitation,
she remembered she was purchased with great price

"All we like sheep
have gone astray to our own way" (Isa. 53:6).
"Increased with goods" (Rev. 3:17),
we think our hearts cannot be moved.

How quickly we forget
who "made our mountains" (Ps. 30:7)
until like the dove,
we find no place to rest our foot.

Glad we are
for sunshine after a rain,
and thankful for the calm after the storm.
When the Tree of Life extends His branch to reach us,
no better rest awaits our guilty souls.

~~~~

"All who are heavy laden, come (Matt. 11:28),
a broken, contrite heart, I won't despise" (Jer. 3:12).
No need to bring an olive branch back with you,
"Return to Me, and I'll return to you" (Mal. 3:7).

Samuel

Wherefore it came to pass when the time was come about after Hannah had conceived, that she bare a son, and called his name Samuel, saying, Because I have asked him of the LORD.

—1 Samuel 20:19

I t is good to rise early and find a quiet place to commune with God. Though many times we have just reason to have a troubled spirit, it should not divert us from our attention to holy things.

Hannah knew this well. Her heart grieved because the "Lord had shut her womb" (1 Sam. 1:5). Though she was overwhelmed with sorrow, she was not embittered to be unthankful, nor was she forgetful of other comforts. "God has set the one over-against the other" (Eccl. 7:14), Solomon writes, and so should we.

Known for her quiet spirit, Hannah had seemingly unwavering faith despite her circumstances, and the fruit of her mouth and the meditations of her heart were acceptable in God's sight (Ps. 119:14). Every year as she went up to the house of the Lord, her adversary, the devil, "provoked her sore" (1 Sam. 1:6), causing her to "weep and not eat (1 Sam. 1:7). "I am a woman of a sorrowful spirit," she said to Eli, "but I have poured out my soul before the Lord" (1 Sam. 1:15).

The answer to Hannah's prayer is a beautiful testimony of how the Lord honors His promises. "Elkanah knew Hannah, his wife, and the LORD remembered her" (1 Sam. 1:19). Months later, she bore him a son and "called his name, Samuel, saying, "Because I have asked him of the Lord" (1 Sam. 1:20).

Hannah, did you talk with God each day,
and did you surely say:
"Lord, unto You I lift my voice,
and for a son, I pray"?

When you rose to your feet,
did you not once doubt
that God would hear your prayers,
or did you always believe you would conceive
the fruit of your earnest words?

How did you know on your blessing day,
that Samuel was his name?
Did you know that his name means:
"God has heard,"
when on wings of prayer, He came?

Lord,

You may not readily answer our prayers, but how strikingly punctual You are to attend to us when we call upon Your Name. We don't always know how to pray as we ought, but we acknowledge and are thankful that You know what we need before we ask.

Speak to My Heart, O God

Whom have I in heaven but thee? There is none
upon the earth that I desire beside Thee?

—Psalm 73:25

Jesus rose a great while before day and "withdrew into the wilderness to pray" (Lk. 5:16). These early retreats provided time away from the crowds to communicate privately with His Father. May our early mornings with Jesus do the same.

Whom have I in heaven, but Thee?
For I, "bought with a price" (1 Cor. 6:20)
am not my own.

Speak to my heart, O God,
that place unheard by any ear, but mine.
Your gentle voice brings peace
the world can't comprehend

Light a candle in my soul that I might sing:
"Spring up! O well" (Num. 21:17)
until the day the shadows flee away.

Lord,

How can we live joyfully, or live at all, if we have no assurance that our life is in You, and our support, Your undertaking? Teach us to "walk circumspectly, not as fools, but as wise, redeeming the time, for the days are evil" (Eph. 5:15,16), and keep us mighty in prayer that we may speak Your Word in due season.

Such Winnowed Wheat

These were more noble than those in Thessalonica in that they
received the word with all readiness of mind and searched
the scriptures daily, whether those things were so.

—John 5:39

How so, the natural man cannot perceive the Word of God? It
is foolishness to "the unlearned" and "hard to understand"
(2 Pet. 3:16). All praise is due our Savior, who "opened up
our understanding" (Lk. 24:45), and in whose name we pray: "Give
us an understanding heart."

Such winnowed wheat we find
in God's great granary!

This Bread of Life is ours—
the purest milk for babes and meat for men.

No royal chariot, bejeweled,
nor spec of gold,
outshines the wisdom found within.

Page-by-page, it testifies of Christ,
the Alpha and Omega—
in whose blood, we are forgiven.

Lord,

Nothing gives us strength or affords guidance, as does prayer.
Impart in us an understanding heart and wisdom to speak to all
whose hearts You've made ready for seed. Keep us true to Your
truths as we gain depth, which cannot come from any other source.

The Beacon

Lead me in Your truth, and teach me: for You are the
God of my salvation; on You do I wait all the day.

—Psalm 25:5

The mountain of Shénir shimmers in its stead, as the shadows on the foothills raise their shades. Looking west of the sunrise toward the sound of a whistle, we decide to board the early morning train.

As the engine twists and turns its way through the shimmering streams of the foothills, it reminds us of the song, "Spring up, O Well" (Num. 21:17) —the song Israel sang near the brooks of Ar, where the LORD spoke unto Moses, saying, "Gather the people together, and I will give them water to drink" (Num. 21:16).

The whistle signals a stop, but before we disembark, we say a prayer to the Lord: "Set a watch, O God, before our mouths, and keep the door of our lips, so that our prayers come before You like incense and the lifting of our hands as the evening sacrifice" (Ps. 141:2,3). When the train slows to a stop, we see a lighthouse keeping watch over the Atlantic—a reminder that "nothing is covered that shall not be revealed, nor hidden that shall not be known" (Lk. 12:2).

Standing on the dock is a man dressed in simple garments calling out to passersby: "This day is holy to the Lord: mourn not, nor weep, but go your way, eat the fat, and drink the sweet. Send portions unto them for whom nothing is prepared, for this day is holy unto the Lord; neither be ye sorrowful, for the joy of the Lord, is your strength" (Neh. 8:9,10). As we go about our days heeding the words of the Lord, we experience the joy of which this man spoke about.

You are the reason
for a miracle that's happening
and the Voice that says it's going to be alright—
the Light of the World,
The Dayspring from on high,
and the bright and Morning Star that gives us life.

You are the angel watching when we're unaware,
and the stranger that appears along the way.
Like an owl of the desert,
You keep watch over us,
and on You, do we wait all the day.

Thank You for Your promise in the rainbows—
unspoken memorandums in skies of grey.
Thank You for Your Word that safely guides us
as a lamp unto our feet to light our way.

The Early Drops of Rain

Watchman, what of the night? Watchman, what of the night?
—Isaiah 21:11

T he night watchman stands ready on the walls of Jerusalem in times of war to answer the man of Mount Seir: "Morning comes, but also night. If you would inquire, inquire; then, come back again" (Isa. 21:12). Likewise, the watchman of the house keeps a lookout for a thief and stands ready so that his house is not broken into.

As we begin to feel the *early drops of rain,* we, too, stand penitent before the Lord, asking: "What of the night?" (Isa. 21:11). "As lightning that comes from the east is visible even in the west, so will be the coming of the Son of Man" (Matt. 24:27). Those who are wise will have their lamps filled with oil. "Blessed is he who watches and keeps his garments ready" (Rev. 16:15).

"What of the night?"
I asked the watchman of the camp.
I did not hear the trumpet
warning of the time at hand.

"The hour is now," he said to me,
"to wake up and repent,
for this, I know, the Master comes
at an hour we least expect" (Mk. 13:35).

"The morning comes," he cautioned me,
"like a thief comes in the night" (1 Thess. 5:2).

I urge you to be ready,
putting on the armor of Light."

"What of the night?" I asked again,
while penitent I be,
for I discerned the time was nearer
than when I first believed (Rom. 13:11).

"You discern foul weather," the watchman said,
"but not the signs of the times?" (Matt. 16:3).
"When the branch is tender and puts forth leaves,
you know that summer is nigh" (Matt. 24:32).

Be not as one without the oil
before the Master came,
knowing that the time was near
by the early drops of rain.

Lord,

We rise early to seek You. As we come into Your presence,
anoint us with oil and trim our lamps so that we are ready to greet
You when You step out on a cloud.

The Good Shepherd

The Lord is my Shepherd; I shall not want. He makes me lie
down in green pastures: He leads me beside the still waters.

—Psalm 23:1,2

W ho is not comforted as he reads: "The Lord is my
Shepherd?" There is nothing like this truth found in the
Word of God, and happy are those who, while searching
the scriptures, find "the Good Shepherd who gave His life for the
sheep" (Jn. 10:11).

We recognize our need for God while daily sitting at the Lord's
table, and each day our love for Him grows deeper as He sends us a
fresh supply of heavenly grace. Our fluttering hearts are not a quiet
emotion but all-consuming energy that shines on our faces as the
Holy Spirit reveals Himself to us.

We are blessed to stand unpunished before a Holy God and to
"know the love of Christ, which passes knowledge, that we might be
filled with all the fullness of God" (Eph. 3:19) treasured up in Christ
Jesus. Those who know the Lord boldly exclaim, "I shall not want,"
trusting Him to supply their every need.

Morning prayer is a sweet beginning as they feed on the Bread
of Life and taste of His goodness; finding His green pastures
nourishment enough, they no longer desire the things of the world.

All good things come through Jesus Christ in whose hand are
all abundant treasures. He knows our sitting down and our rising,
and "neither is there any creature that is not manifest in His sight"
(Heb. 4:13).

The stars may go out at night, but the Good Shepherd is by our
side to guide us continually and to "deliver us from the snare of the
fowler" (Ps. 91:3). As we go out today to proclaim the gospel of Jesus
Christ, may all such comforting words be reserved for such a loving
Benefactor!

Good Shepherd,
how can it be that You are tried,
and I go free to lie down in Your pastures
of fertile fields of green?

Like a deer panting for water,
I thirst for You, O God—
"The One who is, and who was,
and the One who is to come" (Rev. 1:4).

In You, I have all that I need,
and never shall I want,
except that all the earth may know,
O God, how great You are!

Lord,

"Intreat me not to leave You, nor to cease from following after You: for where You go, I will go, and where You lodge, I will lodge" (Ruth 1:16-17).

The Lifter of My Head

But not long after, there arose against it a tempestuous
wind, called "Euroclydon." And when the ship was caught,
and could not bear up into the wind, we let her drive.

—Acts 27:14

I t is good to abound in the company of those whose source of
joy is the Lord and to have faithful friends who will pray with
us in times of need. Even Jesus, "being in agony, prayed more
earnestly, and there appeared an angel unto Him from heaven to
strengthen Him" (Lk. 22:43,44).

"We are troubled on every side, yet not distressed; we are
perplexed, but not in despair" (2 Cor. 4:8,9); those who 'sow in
tears shall reap in joy'" the psalmist writes (Ps. 126:5). Happy is he
who considers Christ's work on the cross clear proof of His Father's
intention to fulfill His Word.

Dear Lord,
I need You once again;
You are my hope when all is gone.
Undone, with dreams, defeated—
in brokenness, I come.

God of the sparrow when it falls—
in whom my help comes from,
only You can stop the rain
and calm "Euroclydon" (Acts 27:14).

Mourning finds me looking
to the "lifter up of my head" (Ps. 3:3),
where I'm reminded of Your promise
in the rainbow that You made.

My face begins to smile again,
and my heart begins to pound,
as You bring good tidings unto me
from high above the mount!

"Amazing Grace," I hear—
as if Your opened arms could sing.
Oh, what a song to love, O God,
when nothing's left of me.

Lord,

Though seasons change or You reverse the tides, You are with us and hear our prayers. Your mighty hand may make our world a humble place, but You keep our burdens light enough to bear; You love us more than we can ever know, and You're the One whom death and hell cannot restrain. When nothing is left, You are there to pick us up; You loves us through the storm, and You are "the lifter of our heads" (Ps. 3:3). Hope is restored when we fall into the arms of the One who is alive and the One who never dies.

The Place No Vanity Allures

Isaac went out to meditate in the field at the eventide: and he
lifted his eyes, and saw, and behold, the camels were coming.

—Genesis 24:63

W hat a beautiful setting for Isaac to converse with God and
find rest for his soul. Like a zealous watchman looking
out from the tower of Jezreel, he waits for the Lord to
answer his prayers.

Isaac's believing expectations are not disappointed. Looking up
from his repose, he sees the answer to his prayer riding on the back
of a camel; by the hand of God, he and Rebekah are brought together.

How big is God, and is He "able to do exceedingly abundantly
above all that we ask or think" (Eph. 3:20)? Out of the midst of the
darkness, we hear the voice of the Lord: "Be still and know" (Ps. 46:10).

With breathtaking wonder, we watch as He calls the stars by
name, bringing "out their hosts by number" (Isa. 40:26). He tells the
moon to stand still in its season, and "the sun knows his going down"
(Ps. 104:19). "God is in the heights of the heavens," we exclaim,
"Behold the heights of the stars, how high they are" (Job 22:12)!
While counting them one by one, we hear the nocturnal call of the
nightingale; beautiful is her song in this late hour.

No hour so peacefully befriends meditation like that of the
evening, and while the heavens declare the glory of God, we find
solace in the company of our Creator.

No study room compares
to walks in fields at eventide—
the place no vanity allures.

With God's creation as our text,
His evening masterpiece unfolds—
unbound by books or painted rooms.

The music of it all one can't compose,
for even marching trebled staffs
can't outperform a closing trumpet-vine,
a lightning bug, or dropping cloud.

No choicest hour remains for yielded souls at rest,
or cattle on a thousand hills to chew their cud.

As nightfall brings surrender to the day,
down on bended knee, we fall,
where His unfailing mercy rests our soul.

Lord,

We lift our eyes above the hills from where our help comes. "Our help comes from You, O God, who made heaven and earth" (Ps. 121:1,2).

The Stone is Rolled Away!

O death, where is your sting? O grave, where is your victory?
—1 Corinthians 15:55

Upon the first day of the week, early in the morning, they came unto the sepulcher, bringing the spices they had prepared and certain others with them. And they found the stone rolled away from the tomb. And they entered in and found not the body of the Lord Jesus. And it came to pass, as they were much perplexed thereabout, behold, two men stood by them in shining garments. And as they were afraid, and bowed down their faces to the earth, they said unto them, Why seek the living among the dead? He is not here but is risen. —Luke 24:1-6

"O death,
where is your sting?" (1Cor. 15:55)
Though you wield your ax
upon the godliest of friends,
your puny power has no affect!

The bonds of death are loosed,
and Christ has plucked your deadly sting!
"Hiss! Hiss!" you cry,
for Jesus Christ has conquered sin
and spoiled the grave!

What say you now, defeated one?
Your cheeks are pale

and how your poisonous darts do sorely grieve!
Betray the Son of man with just a kiss?
Void of understanding, you must be!

While broken stones of law lay in defeat,
the Savior's stone is rolled away
with His redemptive power,
letting the dead in Christ arise!
"Let these go their way," He said (Jn. 18:8).

Resigned to You, O Death—
and that, by His own power, too,
the Savior sweat great drops of blood (Lk. 22:4).

Now, Godly friends shall meet again
someday in heavenly places.

"O grave, where is your victory?" (1 Cor. 15:55).

The Testimony of the Lord

And now unto Him who is able to do exceeding,
abundantly above all that we ask or think.
—Ephesians 3:20

C hristian, are you troubled on every side? Come with me to a higher place, for nothing is more reassuring than a stroll in the evening to be reminded that God can "do exceeding, abundantly above all that we ask or think" (Eph. 3:2). Straight away, you will find yourself nodding to His grace as you listen to His voice on the waters, watch Him cover the heavens with the clouds, prepare the earth for rain, and make the grass grow upon the mountains (Ps. 147:8).

When our confidence shakes to and fro,
we should not fear,
for though we hear the whispering of uncertainty,
"the Testimony of the Lord is sure" (Ps. 19:7)!

While speaking to ourselves in psalms and hymns,
the Word of God suspends uncertainties,
as through the eyes of faith,
we see Eternal things—
"The things which are not seen" (2 Cor. 4:18).

On the day He calls our name,
while Heaven bound, we'll sing:

Jerusalem! Jerusalem!
Cast up, cast up the highway;
gather out the stones (Isa. 62:10)!
You are a city not forsaken,
sought out, and called, "Redeemed" (Isa. 62:12).

Jerusalem! we'll sing,
I'm on my way to see:
The One announced by angels (Lk. 2:11);
the One known by a leper (Matt. 8:2);
the One proclaimed by Jesus (Matt. 21:5),
and He who is Exalted (Acts 5:31).

And in eternity, with certainty,
we shall echo a refrain:

"You are! You are!
You are! You are! You are!"

Lord,

Those who enter into Your rest put thoughts of tomorrow and endless searching far from them. May our hearts be restful and our spirits joyful, as at Your feet, we lay our burdens down.

There is No Love Like His

For as the earth brings forth her bud, and as the
garden causes the things that are sown in it to spring
forth; so the Lord GOD will cause righteousness and
praise to spring forth before all the nations.

—Isaiah 61:11

You are given a seed and instructed to plant it in a place where it will grow steadfast, immovable, and always abounding in the work of the Lord. Where will you plant such a new beginning? One thing is sure: you must place it in fertile ground, where it may be rooted and grounded in love, and where it may grow in the knowledge of our Lord and Savior, Jesus Christ.

O myrtle tree,
What sweet a bloom is earned
while adverse winds
rock you back and forth to try your root!

When drops of rain from darkened clouds
begin to fall in ordered step,
know that God commissioned them for you!

There is no love like His
as little drops of heaven fall your way
and He remembers you.

While His bread of life pours down,
spread your sweet perfume with blooms
beyond all counting!

When the rain is over,
feel your branches reaching high
unto the best rooms in the house,
when like a hart panting for water,
you thirst for more!

One other thing, O bloom,
though distance lies between,
The Lord is able, still,
to look down from the heavens upon you!

Lord,

We begin each day rising before dawn to seek Your face and to meditate in Your promises. Relying on Your guiding hand to lead us, fill us with joy in Your presence, that we may go about our days singing from gladness of heart.

There Stood by Me, an Angel

*There stood by me this night the angel of God, whose I am, and
whom I serve, saying, Fear not, Paul; You must be brought before
Caesar: and God has given you all them that sail with you.*

—Acts 27:23

While on his way to Italy, on storm-tossed seas, Paul sailed
aboard a ship of Alexandria. With circumstances good
and bad, he warned the voyage could take their lives, yet
on they sailed and met the wind, "Euroclydon."

With raging winds to drive the ship
and anchors loosed as violent waves demand,
they made toward shore.

But in the place where two seas meet,
the ship was caught,
and so, instead, they ran aground.

Two hundred three-score sixteen souls
sailed aboard that ship—
some trusting in the captain at the helm.

But, Paul, a servant of the Lord,
heard from God:
"Stay with the ship and live" (Acts 27:31)!

Immovable, the ship stuck fast—
the hinder part did break;
afterward, he took the bread
and thanked the Lord (Acts 27:35).

Trusting God where anchors could not hold,
on broken boards, they sailed.

Fearing they should fall upon the rocks,
there stood by Paul an angel (Acts:27:3)
while safe to shore on broken pieces,
they did ride.

Lord,

When "neither sun nor stars in many days appear and hope that we are saved is gone" (Acts 27:20), whatever course You navigate, we'll take no notice of the rising or the falling of the waves. Like Jacob, with no pillow but a stone (Gen. 28:18) and Your children with no cover but a cloud (Ex. 13:21), You are the Master of our sails. Even if there is no view of the shore in sight, we will trust You, Lord, to bring us safely home.

This Garden Place

And the Lord God called unto Adam, and said unto him,
Where art thou?

—Genesis 3:9

Imagine being placed in a beautiful garden where every tree that is pleasant to the sight and good for food is growing. The tree of life is in the midst and the tree of the knowledge of good and evil. "Of every tree of the garden, you may freely eat, but of the tree of the knowledge of good and evil, you shall not eat, for in the day that you eat thereof, you shall surely die" (Gen. 2:16,17). What will you do?

"Eden," it was called—
the place old age would never know,
where simple was sufficient,
"and man became a living soul" (Gen. 2:7).

The tree of life was in the midst
assuring of immortal life,
but only total acquiesce
secured this earthly paradise.

God took the man and placed Him there
—formed only out of common clay—
He told the man to keep this place
He had created that third day.

Where was this place where streams abound—
where they divide and reunite?

Was it along the Tigris Run
where fruitful trees could please the eye?

Could it be near Mount Shénir,
or there, beside the Caspian Sea
fully adorned by God alone—
this garden place where life was free?

—where Adam heard, "Where art thou?"

Lord,

We are Yours only because You have redeemed us and called us by name. Weigh us in Your balances, and if You should find us wanting, lead us "in the paths of righteousness" and "restore our souls" (Ps. 23:3), so our hearts are not hardened to go our own way.

Unto a Certain Place

Blessed are they who are persecuted for righteousness'
sake: for theirs is the kingdom of heaven.
—Matthew 5:10

S torms can bring the wind, causing waves that make even the
most seaworthy vessel want to kick against the goads. Without
notice, the ship can find itself at the mercy of the tides while
anchored peacefully in the bay. The same is true for a Christian.
Many times, we find ourselves persecuted by wicked men, hurling
stones like hooks to Leviathan.

I went unto a certain place
and observed the cedars of Lebanon.
There, my eyes pour out tears unto God,
and with a heavy heart, I prayed.

"Some suffer for the sake of Christ (Phil. 1:29),
and others without a cause,
but You are a refuge for us all.

Like the birds that make their nests
in the cedars full of sap,
under the shadow of Your wings, I take refuge
until this oppression is over-past."

Afterward,
like the city with no need of the sun (Rev. 22:5),
the light of the Lord appeared through the cedars
and enlightened my soul:

"You who are afflicted—
tossed with tempests,
My eyes are upon their ways (Jer. 16:17).
Take My yoke upon you, and learn of Me,
and you will find rest for your souls" (Matt. 11:29).

Like a tree planted by the waters,
I extend my "roots by the river" (Jer. 17:8),
my leaves are now green, and I no longer fear
when the heat comes.

Lord,

Comfort us with Your presence in times of aggression, sending seasons of refreshing to those who love You. May every form of oppression and wickedness be silenced, so that the whole earth is filled with Your glory.

We, Too, Were Lost

And the angel said unto him, Gird yourself, and bind
on your sandals. And so he did. And he saith unto
him, Cast thy garment about thee, and follow me.

—Acts 12:8

In times past, we had our conversations in the lust of our flesh,
fulling the desires of the flesh and the mind, and we were by nature
the children of wrath (Eph. 2:3). As Christians, we still wrestle with
the old nature, because the flesh lusts against the Spirit and the Spirit
against the flesh (Gal. 5:17). However, with the Captain of our salvation
on our side, we are "more than conquerors" (Rom. 8:37), for He is more
than a match for the enemy.

It's hard to court the world
where sin runs free as if there were no bounds
and live in peace
within the bounds of God.

We must not let
the world, the flesh, and the devil,
bring occasions for repose,
nor should we dare to dabble there.

Let him who reads this understand:
The time of figs has not yet come,
for blind though they may be,
there are those who still remain
who shall believe.

Though this old world is rough-and-tumble,
before we groan among ourselves and pray:
"Come, Lord!"

Remember this:

We, too, were lost,
and barren in the knowledge
of our Lord and Savior, Jesus Christ,
until we bound our sandals on
to follow Him.

Lord,

As we come down the mountain to share the gospel, lead us to those whose hearts you've made ready for seed, and may all who hear of Your good pleasure be willing to bind on their sandals and follow You.

Who Can, like He Can?

Great is Your faithfulness.

—Lamentations 3:23

Nothing is more rewarding than to enjoy the gentle breeze of a cool mountain morning to meditate on Jesus' amazing love. Sitting in His presence banishes everyday worry and weariness. Would that, just like we are buried with Christ in baptism, we might also seek inward spiritual grace, being dead to the world but alive unto the service of God.

Who can
Count the dust of Jacob (Num. 23:10),
call the stars, each one, by name (Isa. 40:26),
make His mercies new each morning (Lam. 3:23),
and in due season, bring us rain (Lev. 26:4)?

Deliver up the poor and needy (Ps. 40:17),
know each sparrow when it falls (Matt. 10:29),
mend the middle wall between us (Eph. 2:14),
and hear our prayers before we call (Isa. 65:24)?

Make us perfect, established, strengthened (1 Pet. 5:10),
give us hope even in death (Prov. 14:32),
restore the year's locusts have eaten (Joel 2:25),
and father, those now fatherless (Ps. 68:5)?

Hear our voices in the morning (Ps. 5:3),
answer, saying: "Here I Am" (Isa. 58:9),
never leave us, nor forsake us (Heb. 13:5),
and give us an expected end (Jer. 29:11)?

Make us lie down in green pastures (Ps. 23:2),
lift all those who are bowed down (Ps. 146:8),
bear our grief, and carry sorrows (Isa. 53:4),
and make us hear the joyful sound (Ps. 89:15)?

Give us food when we are hungry (Ps. 146:7),
keep our feet on solid ground (Ps. 116:8),
put our tears into His bottle (Ps. 56:8),
and comfort those of us who mourn (Isa. 61:2)?

Bear our cross unto Golgotha (Jn. 19:17),
show the nail scars in His hand (Jn. 20:27),
give His life for all the world (Jn. 3:16),
and say, "Forgive them" (Lk. 23:34)
like He can?

Wisdom Stood Upon the Shore

Behold, You desire truth in the inward parts: and in the
hidden part, You shall make me know wisdom.

—Psalm 51:6

It is breathtaking to look out across the vast expanse of the
mountains; the heavens laugh, as their grandeur shows us our
insignificance. Keenly aware of our nothingness in comparison,
we appreciate their beauty and know they exists only by divine
appointment.

Wisdom cried out in high places,
above the heights of Mt. Tabor;
nearer still, wisdom stood,
as we brought fishing boats to shore.

"Gennesaret," the lake was called,
where wisdom stood upon the shore—
the morning Jesus came to us
while in mere fishing boats, we were.

We knew Him in the Synagogue,
but there, we recognized Him not.
"Children, have you any meat?" He asked (Jn. 21:5),
We answered: "No," for we had naught.

When from the shore of Galilee,
"Let down your nets" (Lk. 5:4), He said to me.
Shoals of fish swam to our net—
One hundred fifty and the three! (Jn. 21:11).

How can we gaze into the night
and watch God make His wisdom known,
but when the night is over,
know Him not at early morn?

And who knows not His presence
in quiet places of the heart,
while there He tucks His wisdom
down inside this hidden part (Ps. 51:6)?

Lord,

Drawing near to You and desiring Your truth brings "peace within our walls and prosperity within our palaces" (Ps. 122:7). Help us not to live as one who does not know You, but as one "accepted in the beloved" (Eph. 1:6).

You are Not Saved?

The harvest is past, the summer is ended, and we are not saved.
—Jeremiah 8:20

Thinking back over the years, I recall the days I did not know my Maker's ways—a time when each moment seemed only to be eaten up by the grasshopper and the cankerworm. All of us have been that certain man who had a fig tree planted in his vineyard and who sought fruit thereon, yet found none.

Have you wandered away from God only to find yourself forgotten and alone? And did I hear you say you are not saved? How long before you turn to the Lord, that He may lift Your countenance and give you peace? "Come unto Me, all you who labor and are heavy-laden," He says to you and me, "and I will give you rest" (Matt. 11:28).

Today, if you hear His voice, don't turn away from the One who saved you, for when you do, Jesus Christ, whom you reject, will say unto you in the last days, "Depart from Me, I never knew you" (Jn. 12:32).

The seasons come and go—
"The harvest is past; the summer has ended" (Jer. 8:20).
And the seasons may not come this way again.

But did I hear you say:
"I am not saved"?

Please don't be like those
who run escaping for their lives
and who "run into the caves in fear of God" (Isa. 2:19).

Come with me, instead,
and "let us worship and bow down;

let us kneel before the Lord our God,
and Maker" (Ps. 95:6).

Together, let us pray:
"Dear God,
forgive us of our sins
and cleanse us
from all unrighteousness" (1 Jn. 1:9).

"Lead us in the way, O God,
the way that's everlasting,
so we may be the people of Your pasture.

O Lord, we only want to be,
Yes, Lord, O please just let us be,
Your people, and the sheep of Your hand."

You Shall Be My Guide

"Be of good cheer: for there shall be no loss of any man's
life among you but of the ship. For there stood by me this
night, the angel of God, whose I am, and whom I serve.

—Acts 27:23

Every step of the way, we are assured that our hope is found
in the Lord Jesus Christ. "It is He that forms the mountains,
and creates the wind, and declares unto man what is his
thought. The Lord, The God of hosts, is his name" (Amos 4:13). He
"understands our thoughts afar off" (Ps. 139:2), and there is not a
"creature that is not manifest in His sight" (Heb. 4:13). Even "the little
foxes that spoil the vines" (Song 2:15) cannot hide from the LORD
who "looks from Heaven and beholds the sons of men" (Ps. 33:13).

Compelled to cast ourselves on God alone,
what kind of crashing wave wrecks a man
on such a Rock as this?

When our storm-tossed ship
finds its helmsman trusting in the Lord,
no greater joy remains!

When I, a Mariner,
am lost without a compass,
"with Your counsel,
You shall be my guide" (Ps. 73:24).

Like a blind man
leaning on a friend in need,

"with Your right hand,
You hold on to me" (Ps. 73:23).

So, tempest-tossed believer,
when your ship has run aground
"where two seas meet" (Acts. 27:41),
set the Lord before you, always,
and say like Paul:

"There stood by me, an Angel" (Acts. 27:23).

Lord,

"My voice shalt You hear in the morning, O LORD; in the morning will I direct my prayer unto You and will look up" (Ps. 5:3).

Lord,

At the dawn of each new day,
I will face whatever comes,
and no matter if it rains
I'll be Your audience of one.

If this old world should fade away
while I am standing on this Rock,
You are my "sun and shield" (Ps. 84:11)
that I may stand, no matter what.

Remind me lest I slip,
or I should have a heart of fear,
it's your grace on a wooden cross
that keeps me standing here.

Assure me, too, that I'm redeemed,
and it's You who pleads my cause (1 Jn. 2:1).
If not in You, whom can I trust (Isa. 36:5)
for it is You who gave Your all.

When my death does surely come,
You'll find me here no matter what,
and it will be Your hand I reach for
with everything, I've got.

Even so, come, Lord Jesus. AMEN
—Revelation 22:20

In this pendulum of time, I look from mountains
and gaze out from the heights of Mount Shénir.
While standing on this mountain of the leopards,
I can see the lions' dens from here.

From its peak, I see the summit of Mount Gilead,
the Jordan valley, and the Sea of Galilee.
As nightfall brings the dew atop Mount Tabor,
I'm reminded of the time the Lord was here.

It was evening on the plateau of Mount Hermon,
set apart with only Peter, James, and John,
when Jesus was transfigured there before them,
and His raiment turned exceeding white as snow.

How I wish that I had been there on that mountain
the night when Holy Scriptures were fulfilled—
atop the Mountain of Transfiguration,
where His face shined like the sun upon that hill.

I would listen to the Voice that spoke from heaven
and see the tabernacles made of clouds—
hear Mount Hermon
and Mount Tabor, there, rejoicing,
and stand beside the Lord upon that mount.

A Look From the Top of Shénir Mountain
brings me closer, Lord, to Thee,
to a place the heavens praise Your wonders,
and I can hear You say, "I am with thee."

About the Author

Marilyn Dworshak earned a Master of Business Administration and graduated with Distinction from Keller Graduate School of Management, Houston, TX. She is a published, award-winning Christian author, and Her devotional poetry and prose are held in high regard among religious literature, receiving 2nd and 3rd place awards at statewide Christian Writer's Conferences.

Using her strong understanding of biblical concepts, Marilyn is able to reach across audience's using analogy, word pictures, poetry, and prose tied into devotional commentary to bring words of hope that comfort and encourage.

It is her prayer that all who read *A Look From the Top of Shenir Mountain* will be led to open the Word of God and respond to God's ageless invitation to become a partaker of His divine grace.

Printed in the United States
By Bookmasters